insight text guide

GM Dewis

Dead Poets Society

Dir. Peter Weir

insight™

▶innovative ▶engaging ▶evolving

First published in 2011. Reprinted in 2012, 2018, 2025.

Insight Publications Pty Ltd
3/350 Charman Road
Cheltenham VIC 3192
Australia
Tel: +61 3 8571 4950
Email: books@insightpublications.com.au

www.insightpublications.com.au

National Library of Australia Cataloguing-in-Publication entry:
Dewis, G. M.
Dir. Peter Weir's Dead Poets Society: text guide / GM Dewis.
ISBN 978 1 9214 1105 2 (pbk.)
Weir, Peter, 1944- Dead Poets Society.
Weir, Peter, 1944- –Criticism and interpretation.
Dead Poets Society (Motion picture)
791.4372

Cover design: The Modern Art Production Group

Proudly printed in Australia by Ligare Book Printers

contents

CHARACTER MAP

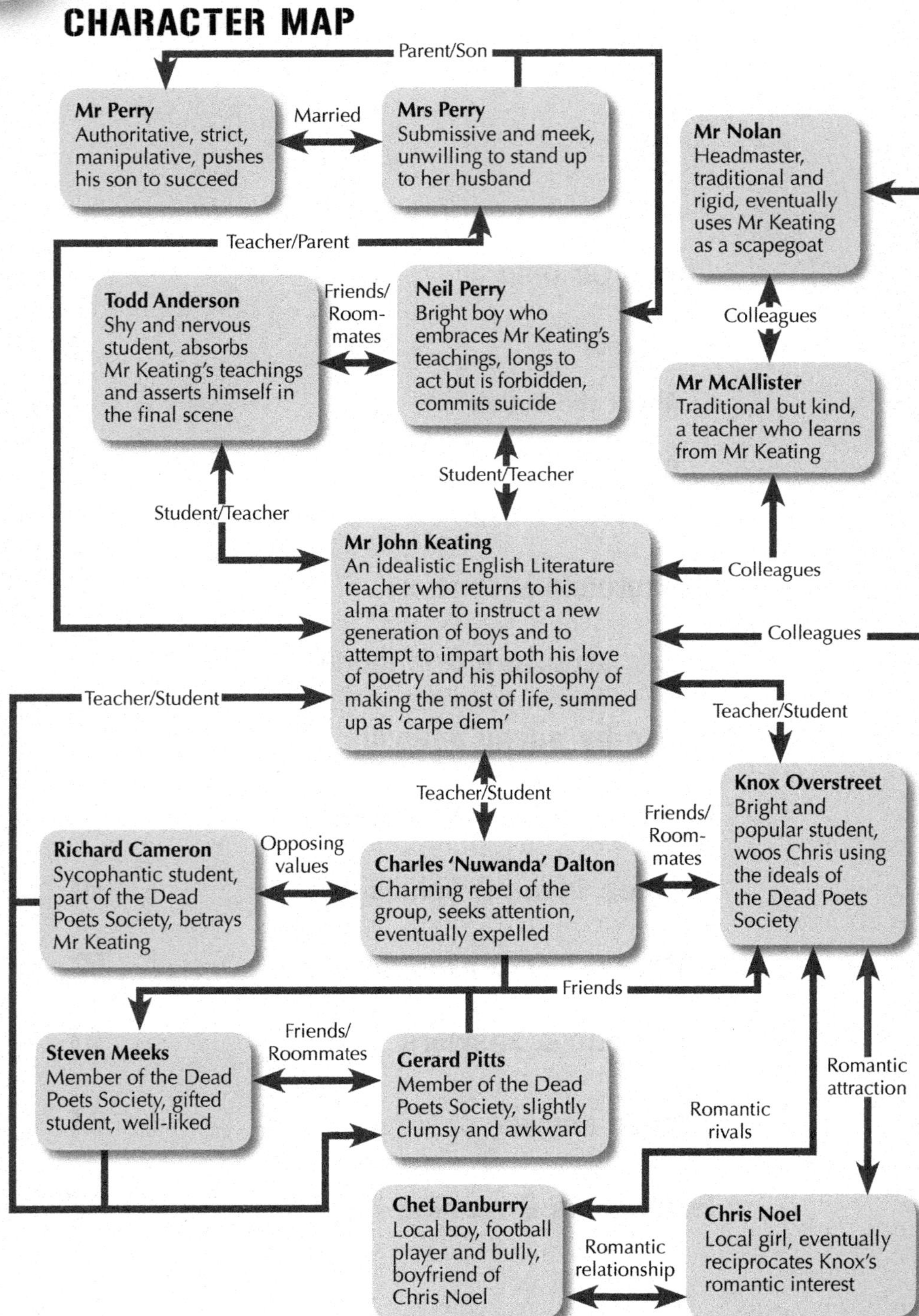

OVERVIEW

About the director

Peter Weir is an Australian director. He has been a significant influence on filmmaking in his native country and his Australian films include *Picnic at Hanging Rock, The Last Wave* and *Gallipoli.* He began his career in television comedy, working on *The Mavis Bramston Show,* before moving on to documentary work with the government-financed organisation Film Australia.

After enjoying significant success in Australia, Weir went on to direct many critically acclaimed international films, including *The Truman Show, Master and Commander* and *Witness* – for which he was nominated for the Academy Award for Best Director. He is also a screenwriter and was nominated for an Academy Award for Best Original Screenplay for the romantic comedy *Green Card* (1990). He also wrote and directed *The Way Back,* a drama set during World War II. Other credits as a director include *The Cars That Ate Paris* and *The Year of Living Dangerously.*

Weir was made a Member of the Order of Australia for his contribution to the arts.

About the screenwriter

Tom Schulman, an American screenwriter, wrote the original screenplay for *Dead Poets Society*, for which he received an Academy Award. Apart from this (his most successful film), Schulman is mainly known for family-friendly films such as *Honey, I Shrunk the Kids* and *What About Bob?*

Synopsis

Set at a fictional boarding school in America in 1959, *Dead Poets Society* tells the story of the arrival of a new, innovative teacher, John Keating, and the effect his personality and teaching methods have on his students. Welton Academy is a prestigious school and its students are expected to attain high grades and graduate into fields such as medicine, finance and law. Self-expression is discouraged, being seen as frivolous, and discipline is strict. Mr Keating encourages students to think for themselves, which has both positive and negative consequences. The two main characters, Neil and Todd, are outwardly very different but inwardly both are passionate and artistic young men. They deal with their desires very differently and, when a death occurs, the teachers, parents and students are left with the difficult task of assigning responsibility.

Character summaries

Mr John Keating

John Keating (played by Robin Williams) is a teacher of English Literature, who has just returned to his boyhood school as a member of staff. His approach to teaching is modern, interactive and intuitive, despite working in a school where traditional, structured and objective methods are considered superior – indeed, the only acceptable methods.

Little is revealed about Mr Keating's personal background, apart from a brief mention (s.9) of a woman (presumably his girlfriend or wife) who is still in England, where he had previously taught. Indeed, his character seems to exist solely in relation to his function as an inspiration to the boys in his class.

John Keating's name is almost certainly a reference to the British poet John Keats, who wrote some of the most famous and emotionally sophisticated poetry of the Romantic period, including such classics as 'Ode on a Grecian Urn' and 'Ode to a Nightingale'. The Romantic period was characterised by a focus on individual feeling and emotional experience. Keats died young (at 26 years old), and is often cited as an artist whose life was tragically cut short, which creates a parallel with the death of Neil in *Dead Poets Society.*

Neil Perry

Neil Perry (played by Robert Sean Leonard) is the son of a middle-class couple who have made significant sacrifices to send their son to Welton Academy. In this sense, he is very different from the privileged boys who attend the school and is under pressure to create a good return on his parents' investment. His father is extremely strict, his mother meek and submissive. While obedient, Neil is also passionate and energetic, and discovers a keen interest in acting during the school year that the film covers, which motivates him to defy his father for the first time. His death by suicide is the climax of the film.

Todd Anderson

Played by Ethan Hawke, Todd is the younger son of a family who has already sent one child to Welton. He is in the shadow of his elder brother (who graduated as valedictorian) and while his parents appear genial, he is extremely meek and shy. His interior life is rich and active, however, and he is drawn to Mr Keating's teachings even though he seems outwardly intimidated. Todd's character arc is one of the most significant features of the film. Most notably, Todd is the first boy to stand on his desk in the final scene, uncharacteristically defying authority and drawing attention to himself, in order to communicate to Mr Keating the positive and transformative impact that his teaching has had.

Mr Perry

Neil's father is played by Kurtwood Smith. A self-made man, Mr Perry is extremely strict, even given the historical context of 1959, the year in which the film is set. Depending on the viewer's interpretation, he can be seen either as a manipulative and power-obsessed character who enjoys dominating his son, or a man who, while misguided, is driven by a desire to see his son happy, established and secure in life.

When Neil kills himself, after his father tells him he will be withdrawn from Welton and sent to military school, Mr Perry is genuinely distraught and cries out, 'My son, my son!' (s.9) while holding Neil's body in his arms. However, he appears to be entirely unwilling to accept even the slightest portion of blame for Neil's actions, and pursues punishment for Mr Keating the very next day, implying he places greater importance on vengeance than on mourning.

Knox Overstreet

Knox (played by Josh Charles) is from a wealthy background and is a well-adjusted and well-liked student at Welton. He is mildly sceptical about Mr Keating's teachings until he meets Chris, a girl with whom he falls in love at first sight. He is the student who is most drawn to the aspects of Mr Keating's ideas that deal with romantic love, and he embraces his teacher's philosophy in a positive and appropriate way. He is among the boys who stand on their desks in the final scene.

Charles (Charlie) Dalton

Charlie (played by Gale Hansen) later adopts the name 'Nuwanda'. He is a rebellious and charismatic Welton student, described as being from 'a rich family' (s.9), and is impetuous and charming, often teasing the other boys. Charlie is among the first to embrace Mr Keating's teachings. He shows himself to be both loyal and rash when he punches Cameron for betraying their teacher. Despite his outward confidence, he seems to be unhappy at Welton, attempting to get himself expelled by perpetrating insolent stunts. He is kind to other boys in their times of need, showing that he is more than simply an attention-seeking rebel. He is expelled near the end of the film, after punching Cameron; his final fate is unknown.

Steven Meeks

'Meeks', as he is referred to by the other boys, is played by Allelon Ruggiero. He is the high-achieving academic in the Welton social group (his specialty is Latin, but he also works with Pitts on building a radio, implying well-rounded knowledge). He is good-natured and breaks the stereotype of the 'smart nerd' by joining the other boys in being quite adventurous. One of his lines is, 'I'll try anything once' (s.3). He is among the boys who stand on their desks in the final scene.

Richard Cameron

Cameron, who is always referred to by his surname, is a conservative member of the boys' social group. He is unwilling to break the rules unless under significant peer pressure. He blames Mr Keating for Neil's death and sets in motion the events that lead to the teacher's dismissal. Whether he believes Mr Keating is to blame or is simply desperate to protect himself is unclear. He is considered a traitor by the other boys, even those who eventually sign the document implicating Mr Keating.

In the original screenplay, Cameron was supposed to be one of the boys who, in the final scene, stand on their desks to honour Mr Keating; however, Dylan Kussman, the actor playing Cameron, read the scene and suggested that his character would not be willing to take the risk associated with this act. In the final version, Cameron stays in his seat, with his face turned downwards, implying that, while he is ashamed of his cowardice, he remains steadfast in giving his own well-being priority over doing the right thing.

Mr Nolan

The headmaster (played by Norman Lloyd) is a traditional man. He refers to his love of teaching, and (not unlike Mr Perry) seems to feel that his strict discipline is in the best interest of the students. Following Neil's death, he intimidates the boys into blaming John Keating, and then fires him. Mr Nolan's main concern is the reputation of the school. His view is that boys need to be moulded with a strong hand and that exposing them to the kind of inflammatory and emotional rhetoric that Mr Keating employs will only make them unfocused and destructive. While corporal punishment was not uncommon at the time, Mr Nolan appears to take a particular satisfaction in beating Charlie, who has been insolent. This reinforces the interpretation that he sees boys as wild and untrustworthy, in need of boundaries – and sometimes brutal discipline – in order to become well-adjusted men.

Gerard Pitts

Pitts, as he is known, is a minor character (played by James Waterston) within the central group. He is affable, occasionally providing comic relief, either via jokes about his surname or through his physical awkwardness (he is the tallest and most gangly of the boys). Like the other boys (except for Charlie), he signs the document implicating Mr Keating, but he is also among those who stand on their desks in tribute to their teacher as he leaves the school.

Chris Noel

Chris (played by Alexandra Powers) is a local girl with whom Knox falls in love. She attends a co-educational public school, unlike the main characters. However, it is implied that she is also from a privileged background. Knox first meets her while having dinner with the Danburry family, friends of his parents. Chris is the girlfriend of the Danburrys' son, Chet. Knox immediately falls in love with Chris and tries to woo her away from Chet.

BACKGROUND & CONTEXT

Historical setting

Dead Poets Society is set at the fictional Welton Academy in Vermont, USA, in 1959. At that time, the economy was strong and education was highly valued. Despite widespread prosperity following the end of World War II, American society was also experiencing the anxiety of the Cold War with the Soviet Union and its satellite states. This veneer of prosperity undercut with tension is thematically reflected in *Dead Poets Society*.

It is important to note that Weir chose 1959, rather than earlier in the 1950s, as the historical setting for the film. By 1959, suggestions of social movements to come were beginning to appear in American culture (notably the civil rights and women's rights movements). Weir has chosen to capture American society right at the turning point of a decade of social cohesion and conformity (the 1950s) and a decade of social upheaval and revolution (the 1960s). Much is at stake in maintaining the status quo at Welton, a microcosm of upper-class society, at a time when rumblings of change and upheaval would be threatening the perceived stability of such institutions. For instance, many private schools similar to Welton began accepting female students in the 1960s, and others began to integrate racially.

Significant class issues inform the narrative, too. Unlike more traditional societies (such as those of Britain or India), in the US social status and class can change significantly from one generation to another within a family, depending on individual success or failure. For this reason, the wealthy and/or upper-class parents of Welton students are extremely keen to see their sons succeed and maintain or improve their family's social standing. For this to happen, it is necessary for the boys to be high achievers in school and enter the professional world, preferably (at the time) as lawyers or doctors. In a sense, each boy is not only working to succeed for himself, but also as a representative of his entire family. A student who performs poorly or flouts authority will shame his parents.

Director's historical context

Weir's work on *Dead Poets Society* earned him another nomination for the Academy Award for Best Director (the first was for *Witness*). The film was also nominated for Best Picture and won the award for Best Original Screenplay for writer Tom Schulman. When *Dead Poets Society* was released, Weir was 45 years old.

Throughout the course of his career, Weir became known for giving actors a chance to break out of their typecasting. In *Dead Poets Society*, he cast well-known comedian Robin Williams in the role of John Keating, which required the actor to carry much of the dramatic action and earned him a nomination for the Academy Award for Best Actor. Later in his career, Weir would make a similar casting decision when he chose another comedian, Jim Carrey, to star as the dramatic lead in *The Truman Show*, another film about repressive environments and the indomitable triumph of personal choice.

Weir chose to film *Dead Poets Society* in sequence, unlike most films, hoping that the emotions of the actors would build as their characters experienced intense interior journeys. Robin Williams compared Weir himself to a Mr Keating–like influence and inspiration on the set.

Screenwriter's historical context

Dead Poets Society remains Tom Schulman's most acclaimed work. It is notable that the film was released in 1989, roughly 20 years after Schulman graduated from Montgomery Bell Academy in Nashville, Tennessee, the school upon which he based Welton Academy. The character of John Keating was inspired by one of Schulman's real teachers, Samuel F Pickering Jr, who went on to teach at the University of Connecticut after his brief tenure at Montgomery Bell Academy.

Pickering, for his part, has avoided association with the film, noting that, while he and Keating had similarly unorthodox styles of teaching, his method was less directed by a particular philosophy and more motivated by the simple desire to keep himself and his students interested in the material.

Cinematic historical context

Trends in films during the 1980s include the rising mainstream success of the teen movie. Directors such as John Hughes began to focus on young ensemble casts. In both comedy and drama, films began to be aimed at younger audiences and the themes and actors reflected that trend. Notable examples include *St Elmo's Fire* (1985) and *Footloose* (1984). *Dead Poets Society* follows this trend both by using a young ensemble cast and by concerning itself with themes of particular interest to young people, notably those of identity, conformity and the relationships of the protagonists with authority figures such as their parents and teachers.

Poised on the cusp of two decades, *Dead Poets Society* is also seen to reflect film trends of the 1990s. Serious dramas emerged as particularly popular in the early 1990s, e.g. *Philadelphia* (1993), *Schindler's List* (1993) and *Dances with Wolves* (1990), and films dealing with identity, e.g. *Thelma and Louise* (1991), were also well-supported.

From an industry standpoint, *Dead Poets Society* is in keeping with other films produced by Touchstone (a subsidiary of Walt Disney Pictures), the American studio that distributed the film. Examples of similar Touchstone films include *Remember the Titans* (2000), *Pearl Harbour* (2001), *Rushmore* (1998) and *Beaches* (1988). *Dead Poets Society* continues to be considered one of Touchstone's notable films.

Other significant films released across the industry in 1989, the same year as *Dead Poets Society,* included *Batman; Field of Dreams; Honey, I Shrunk the Kids; Indiana Jones and the Last Crusade; James Bond: License to Kill;* and *The Little Mermaid.*

GENRE, STRUCTURE & LANGUAGE

Genre

Dead Poets Society is, in the most general terms, a drama. It is also a modern historical film, examining the social mores of a time that is familiar to many people alive today. In particular, it is a boarding-school story.

The subgenre of the boarding-school novel or film is well-established. Examples include the novels *Nicholas Nickleby* by Charles Dickens, *A Separate Peace* by John Knowles and *The Catcher in the Rye* by J. D. Salinger, and the films *School Ties, Toy Soldiers* and *Goodbye, Mr Chips* (the latter focusing on school life from the teacher's point of view). Narratives in this genre often involve breaking rules and regulations for noble or individualistic reasons (rather than for personal gain or with bad intentions); a transition from boyhood to manhood; an assertion of independence and, often, the death of a classmate as a transformative and maturing experience.

The role of social and economic class is notable in *Dead Poets Society* as it is in many boarding-school narratives. The boys are expected to matriculate to a US Ivy League University and their career options are often listed as finance, law, medicine and (less frequently) engineering. This focus on the class constraints of the time informs the historical genre of the film.

Structure

The opening and closing scenes are key to understanding the themes of *Dead Poets Society*. In the opening scene, in which Mr Nolan addresses the students and parents, all the main characters are behaving with utter decorum. By the final scene they have broken out of the strict expectations of their social class and their school and asserted their individualism.

There are ten sections on the DVD version of the film. The second-last section, however, is particularly long and is the portion of the film in which much of the action takes place. Weir's decision to slow the narrative timeline down and use the final night of Neil's life as the film's climax highlights the tension and drama of Neil's death. One of the shortest sections, by contrast, is the final section where the boys assert their new-found values of bravery, loyalty and individualism.

The other notable aspect of the structure is the division of the emotional narrative. Whereas most films and books have one central character, *Dead Poets Society* effectively has two or, it can be argued, employs a shift from one character to another, as the main emotional drive of the story. Both Neil and Todd undergo similar journeys of self-discovery, but the outcomes are very different: Neil, in a moment of extreme despair, is pushed to take his own life, while Todd inspires himself to put into practice the ideals he has absorbed from Mr Keating's teaching, symbolically achieving manhood. It is unusual for a filmmaker to focus on two main characters in the manner that Weir has chosen to do, and this lends the film a unique narrative interest for the viewer.

Language

Weir chooses to incorporate into the script significant portions of the poetry being studied in Mr Keating's class. Original compositions are also included, such as John Keating's own (apparently spontaneous) lines spoken to Mr McAllister at dinner (s.3), Knox's poem for Chris (s.6) and Todd's poem about the madman (s.6), composed in class with his eyes closed to dampen his fear of judgment and attention. Charlie, for his part, is often seen taking credit for the poetry of others, as he does in section 7 when reciting poetry (by Byron and Shakespeare) to the girls in the cave, and when he is slow to attribute to Abraham Cowley the poem he reads from the back of the centrefold.

Using the poetry directly, rather than just alluding to it, highlights the importance of literature to the film's theme and arc and also allows viewers to test their own reaction to poetry, just as the boys are doing throughout the film. The quotation from Thoreau's *Walden* lends the film its central message:

> I went to the woods because I wished to live deliberately, to front only the essential facts of life, and see if I could not learn what

it had to teach, and not, when I came to die, discover that I had not lived. (quoted by Neil, s.4)

This piece is particularly central to the film as it not only highlights the importance of self-discovery and individualism, but also foreshadows the death that supplies the climax of the film's action.

Also important to the viewer's experience of language in *Dead Poets Society* is the catchphrase of the film, *'carpe diem'* (Latin for 'seize the day'), which is one of the first lessons Mr Keating imparts to the boys. The phrase becomes a catch-all for the boys to motivate themselves to strive for whatever they desire but have previously been too meek to pursue (acting for Neil, poetry for Todd, romance for Knox). However, the dark side of the *carpe diem* philosophy is highlighted by Neil's suicide: it encourages impetuosity and discourages the boys from taking a long-term view of their actions and desires. It is notable, as well, that the phrase is the only non-English quotation employed. This gives it a mystical quality, like a secret password or magic spell, as well as referencing the boys' education and privilege.

Music

The score of *Dead Poets Society* has a significant influence on how the film is experienced by the viewer. The film opens with ambient sounds rather than music, which reflect the routine and unchanging nature of the school prior to Mr Keating's arrival, as well as an absence (which the school has striven to maintain) of a Romantic atmosphere. Mr Keating first enters the classroom whistling Tchaikovsky's *1812 Overture*, showing that music and art are constant elements in his life. Weir's selection of a Romantic-era composer is no accident. Similarly, there is a short scene (s.6) without any diegetic sound at all (sound whose source is visible on the screen or is implied to be present by the action of the film, such as characters' voices, sounds made by objects or actions), in which the boys play soccer while Beethoven's *Ode to Joy* is heard as non-diegetic sound (i.e. it is implied that the music is not actually being played as part of the action – the boys would not be able to hear it; it is part of the aesthetic of the film). In this scene, the boys are shown as young, healthy and happy and their happiness is connected to Mr Keating, whom they lift onto their shoulders after the game is won.

In general, Weir employs what is called empathetic sound throughout the film, i.e. the choices of music and sound are used to support the emotional mood of a scene rather than to contrast with it (also seen, for example, in Neil's suicide scene). He also notably chooses music by Romantic-era composers in several scenes (Beethoven is considered to be a Romantic-era composer, as is Tchaikovsky). Romantic music is connected thematically with Mr Keating, as his personal philosophy embraces Romantic-era ideals of self-awareness, emotional experience and individualism.

The main theme, played on bagpipes, is one of the more formalised pieces of music; it draws on traditional Scottish folk themes in keeping with the atmosphere of Welton Academy.

Clothing

The boys are seen in uniform almost exclusively throughout the film. This highlights the lack of individualism and self-determinism at Welton Academy, as well as the student's social class. The uniforms are formal and tailored, designed more for appearance than comfort or ease of movement.

Mr Keating dresses less formally than the other teachers, who generally favour three-piece suits. He wears comparatively casual clothes (sports jacket, not a suit) in his final appearance (s.10) when he comes to collect his things.

One of the most thematically significant uses of clothing in the film is the costume Neil wears as Puck in *A Midsummer Night's Dream*. It is the opposite of his school uniform: made to facilitate movement, it is very informal and reveals his body. It is also notable that he removes most of his clothes before shooting himself, implying that clothing represents a certain conformity and imprisonment from which he wants to free himself for one last time.

SCENE-BY-SCENE ANALYSIS

Note: For this guide, the film is divided into ten sections for ease of discussion. The division for the sections, and section titles, are from the chapter divisions on the DVD version of the film. This will facilitate easy reading of the guide and referencing of the film. References are formatted as (s.#), citing the section from which they quote.

Section one: A new semester

The opening scene of *Dead Poets Society* is outside the Welton Academy chapel, where students and their families are having their photographs taken before Mr Nolan, the headmaster, addresses them inside the chapel. The film's title text appears beside a candle, which Mr Nolan says represents the light of learning. However, the candle also represents the vulnerability and intensity of youth.

Four banners, which represent the values of Welton Academy, are carried into the chapel: 'Tradition', 'Honor' *[sic]*, 'Discipline' and 'Excellence'. The first banner we see is 'Discipline', followed by 'Tradition', showing what is most strongly valued at the school.

Neil is seen sitting beside his father, looking tense, while Todd hesitates to stand with the other students, as his father is encouraging him to do. These shots are used to establish the boys' natures and their relationships with their parents.

Mr Keating is introduced and he smiles down the row of teachers, indicating his comparatively warm nature in the very proper and straight-faced environment of the school chapel.

Neil and Todd are both filmed again as they exit with their parents (Neil's mother is notably not present, despite it obviously being common for mothers to accompany the sons and fathers to the school). Mr Nolan tells a visibly nervous Todd he has 'some big shoes to fill' (s.1) as his brother was 'one of our finest', a Welton valedictorian.

When greeting Neil Perry and his father, Mr Nolan expresses high hopes for the boy. Mr Perry says, 'Oh, he won't disappoint us', to which

Neil says, 'I'll do my best, sir' (s.1). This early exchange again cements the viewer's understanding of their relationship.

Outside, Neil approaches Todd and introduces himself, showing himself to be the more interactive of the two.

In the dormitory, all the boys arrive to confirm who will be in their study group. This scene establishes the main characters and the spirit of the social group: jovial, with a sense of camaraderie. Believing their parents have all left, the boys irreverently mock the four pillars of the school, refer to the school as 'Hellton' and smoke in the room, embracing small rebellions that would be within the acceptable limits for upper-year students. They attempt to include Todd in their socialising, but he resists.

Mr Perry arrives unexpectedly in the room and tells Neil, in front of the other boys, that he's taking too many extra-curricular activities, demanding that he drops his involvement in editing the school annual. When Neil protests, his father orders him out of the room and warns him not to defy him, especially in front of others, despite it being Mr Perry himself who began the exchange with others present. This act reveals Mr Perry's manipulative nature. Neil immediately relents and his father adds, before he leaves, 'You know how much this means to your mother' (s.1), attempting to use guilt and shame to cow Neil into submission.

Key point

In this scene, Mr Perry forbids something that Neil values and is attached to, claiming to be doing so in his son's best interest. It is clear he is determined to control every aspect of Neil's life and that, at this point, Neil will inevitably give in to his father in such conflicts.

The boys comfort Neil and encourage him to defy his father. Neil accuses them of being hypocritical, noting they're under similar pressures and that they would never be as rebellious as they are suggesting. They admit this is true.

The following day, a montage shows the boys in various classes, conjugating Latin aloud and receiving strict and heavy workloads. These shots of traditional and structured learning processes are used to contrast with Mr Keating's approach to teaching, which opens the following section.

Q What coping mechanisms does Neil use in this section to deal with his father and how successful are they?

Q Are Todd and Neil presented as opposites or complements in this section?

Section two: Seize the day

In the English classroom, John Keating is seen peering from his office and then enters, whistling the *1812 Overture*, by Romantic-era composer Tchaikovsky. In this way he references his values before he even speaks, as his entire philosophy is based on the tenets of the Romantic Movement.

After leading the boys to the trophy hall, Mr Keating says, 'Oh Captain! my Captain' (s.2) and asks the boys where the quote is from. No one knows so he tells the class it is by American poet Walt Whitman, and refers to President Abraham Lincoln. He invites the students to call him 'O Captain! my Captain!' and then gives a candid speech, referring to the school (which he attended as a young man) as 'Hellton', as the boys do. This serves to establish rapport and also invites the students to relate to their teacher as an equal, an approach that is quite shocking at Welton.

Mr Keating asks Pitts to read the first stanza of the poem 'To the Virgins, to Make Much of Time' by Robert Herrick. Keating summarises the poem's sentiment as *carpe diem*, which Meeks accurately translates from Latin as 'seize the day'. This becomes the film's catchphrase and the mantra of the main characters.

During the discussion, Charlie gives a cheeky answer, in an attempt to test the new teacher. When Mr Keating is unfazed, Charlie is impressed. In this moment he becomes the first boy to openly approve of Mr Keating, which is important as Charlie is charismatic and has a strong influence over the other boys.

Mr Keating then says, 'Each and every one of us in this room is one day going to stop breathing, turn cold and die' (s.2), in an attempt to encourage the boys to value their lives. The camera then shows Neil, who appears uncomfortable. The juxtaposition of the mention of death with the shot of Neil foreshadows his death later in the film.

Asking the boys to look at the photographs of past Welton classes, Mr Keating tells them to consider whether those graduates had 'seized the day' or not. He then whispers, *'carpe diem'*, pretending to be the ghostly voice of past graduates. Reacting to this after Mr Keating has left, Pitts says, 'That was weird' (s.2). Neil however, replies, 'But different' (s.2). Knox chimes in, 'Spooky, if you ask me' (s.2). Cameron's reaction is to ask whether they will be tested on 'that stuff', to which Charlie replies, 'Oh come on, Cameron. Don't you get anything?' (s.2). These reactions are important as they summarise the mindset of each of the characters: Pitts is good-natured but uninterested in the unusual; Neil is longing for something, anything different from his current life; Knox is easily made nervous; Cameron is focused on academic achievement; and Charlie is looking for excitement. This is a narrative shortcut that serves to explain the characters' natures to the viewer in an economical way.

In the locker room, the boys plan their study group and Knox explains that he has to have dinner with the Danburrys, friends of his family. In this scene, Todd, who is still quite separate from the other boys, is fully dressed while the other boys are in towels. He is invited to the study group, but declines. The scene cuts to Todd alone in his room, where he writes 'Seize the day!' in large letters in a notebook. Frustrated, he rips out and crumples up the page, then opens a textbook.

Key point

Showing Todd's reaction individually, rather than including him in the previous scene where all the boys give their reactions one after another, highlights the importance of Todd's character, and also the comparatively internal journey he undertakes.

The scene cuts to a teacher (Dr Hager) driving Knox to the Danburrys' for dinner and there are lingering shots of the school grounds and the surrounding neighbourhood, an idyllic town under a pink sunset. The beautiful pastoral setting implies that all is well, healthy and happy at Welton. Since the viewer knows this is not entirely true (e.g. we are already aware of Neil's frustration with his strict father), the shot is somewhat ironic.

At the Danburry house, Knox is greeted by Chris, the pretty young girlfriend of the Danburrys' son, Chet.

Back at Welton, Knox declares, 'Tonight I met the most beautiful girl I have ever seen in my entire life' (s.2). Knox's romantic nature is revealed with this sudden infatuation. The timing of this meeting makes him receptive to Mr Keating's teachings.

Meeks and Pitts are seen working on building a radio, which is forbidden. This is an example of the smaller, more modest rebellions the boys engaged in prior to Mr Keating's arrival.

Q Why is it important that one of the boys experiences romantic love while in Mr Keating's class?

Q What does it say about the character of Todd that he prefers to write in his notebook about Mr Keating's teachings rather than to discuss them with the other boys? Why is this important to the film's themes?

Section three: Understanding poetry

In English class, opening the poetry textbook, *Five Centuries of Verse*, Mr Keating asks Neil to read from the preface, 'Understanding Poetry' by Dr Pritchard, which presents a traditional, empirical and somewhat passionless approach to studying poetry. Mr Keating follows along, drawing a graph and playing the part of a traditional teacher. The boys begin to wonder if they have misjudged him. Cameron is seen carefully copying the graph down, showing his literal mindset.

After Neil's reading, Mr Keating shocks the boys by calling the preface 'excrement' (s.3). Charlie seems especially impressed and surprised by his approach and, when Mr Keating instructs the boys to tear the preface out of the book, he is the first to do so.

While Mr Keating has disappeared into his office to get a waste-basket, Mr McAllister enters the room and, surprised by the boys' unruly behaviour, shouts at them. When Mr Keating reappears, Mr McAllister leaves politely, obviously flustered.

Key point

This scene contains many of Mr Keating's most thematically significant lines as he attempts to impress upon the boys the importance and relevance of literature, particularly poetry. He says, 'This is a battle, a war, and the casualties could be your hearts and souls' (s.3), and adds, 'Words and ideas can change the world' (s.3).

Mr Keating goes on to attempt to make the boys understand how poetry relates to them in particular, saying:

> I see that look in Mr Pitts' eye, like nineteenth-century literature has nothing to do with going to business school or medical school ... I have a little secret for you ... We read and write poetry because we are members of the human race, and the human race is filled with passion. And medicine, law, business, engineering, these are noble pursuits, and necessary to sustain life, but poetry, beauty, romance, love: these are what we stay alive for ... that you are here ... that life exists. And identity. That the powerful play goes on and you may contribute a verse. (s.3)

Neil is seen to be enraptured by Mr Keating's speech. Todd, on the other hand, is looking down and appears withdrawn.

In the following scene at the high table, Mr Keating and Mr McAllister discuss what happened in Keating's class. McAllister says, 'You take a big risk by encouraging them to become artists, John. When they realise they're not Rembrandts, Shakespeares or Mozarts, they'll hate you for it' (s.3). Keating says he's only trying to encourage free thinking, to which McAllister responds, 'Free thinkers at seventeen?' (s.3), prompting Keating to call him a cynic. This clearly wounds Mr McAllister: he feels his approach is better for the boys, whom he worries Mr Keating will burden with unachievable dreams.

Key point

This debate is one of the central tensions of the film. It questions whether Mr Keating is being overly idealistic in encouraging the students to make literature a central concern in their lives when, inevitably, very few of them will ever have the ability to write poetically.

At their table, the boys are looking at the yearbook they have found, for the year Mr Keating graduated. They are impressed by his listed achievements. Led by Neil, they find Mr Keating on campus, where he is walking and whistling. He ignores them until they address him as 'O Captain! my Captain'. When they ask about the Dead Poets Society, Keating hesitates but then relents and explains what the society was. After he leaves, Neil suggests they reconvene the society that very night. Cameron is reluctant and Charlie mocks him for being cowardly. Neil demands to know who is in, as Dr Hager yells at the boys to get back into school quickly. Pitts and Knox are also hesitant, but finally agree; Knox relents after Charlie advises him that a grasp of romantic poetry might help in his pursuit of Chris, the girl he met at the Danburrys' house.

Inside, as the boys study a map, Todd also declines to join the society despite Neil's fervent plea, finally admitting that he doesn't want to read aloud. Neil offers to see if the other boys will agree to Todd coming and just listening, and goes off to check with them even though Todd asks him not to. This shows kindness on Neil's part, but also a willingness to break rules, even the rules of the Dead Poets Society.

As the boys prepare for bed, Neil finds Todd and tells him, 'You're in' (s.3). Neil then finds a copy of *Five Centuries of Verse* in his room. Seeing that it belonged to John Keating, who has clearly left it there to encourage him to flout the school rules, Neil smiles. The boys sneak out of the building and are seen as dark figures running across the field and through the woods as ominous music plays, foreshadowing the consequences of the Dead Poets Society.

Q Are Mr McAllister and Mr Keating both equally concerned about their students?

Q Why does Todd agree to join the society even when he is nervous about doing so?

Section four: The reconvening of the Dead Poets Society

In the cave that Mr Keating told them about, Neil reconvenes the society. The boys have trouble lighting a fire and Pitts bumps his head.

Key point

The boys' clumsiness and ineptitude is highlighted to represent how unacquainted they are with the natural world, which represents the passionate and Romantic ideals of Mr Keating.

Neil reads from Thoreau, 'I wanted to live deep and suck out all the marrow of life ... and not, when I had come to die, discover that I had not lived' (s.4). Again, this foreshadows Neil's untimely death.

Pitts then reads a poem, after which Charlie stands up, as if he is going to read one of his own. He reads, but the poem (by Abraham Cowley, a seventeenth-century English poet) is written on the back of a pornographic photo, which causes all the boys to cheer. Meeks reads his selection, 'The Congo' by Vachel Lindsay, an American poet whose works were often meant to be chanted or sung. This comparatively modern selection is important in establishing Meeks' character: despite being academically gifted he is not a stereotypical 'brainy nerd'. This shows Weir's desire to go beyond the stereotypical characters of the boarding-school story. The boys then chant, led by Meeks.

Q Why is it important that the setting of the Dead Poets Society be in the natural world and not a classroom or dormitory?

Section five: A different perspective

The next day in class, Mr Keating is speaking to the boys and calls on Todd for a response. When he sees how nervous Todd is, he kindly passes him by rather than forcing him to speak, showing his compassionate nature and innate understanding of Todd in particular.

Mr Keating stands on his desk, to illustrate the importance of perspective. He says, 'Just when you think you know something, you have to look at it in another way, even though it may seem silly or wrong' (s.5). He encourages the boys to put stock in their own opinions and voices. He then has each of the boys stand on his desk and jump off, one after another. For homework, he asks the boys to compose an original poem and says to Todd, 'Mr Anderson, don't think I don't know this assignment scares the hell out of you, you mole' (s.5), then turns out the light, making it more intimidating for Todd, who is on the desk, to step off the edge. So he is seen both being kind to Todd (earlier in the class) and challenging him to break out of his comfort zone.

Key point

Mr Keating's understanding of the boys is essential to the plot; he accurately assesses Todd, but he is inaccurate in his assessment of Neil, with disastrous consequences.

Next there is a montage in which the boys are shown rowing, finishing construction of their radio and fencing. The main purpose of the montage is to show the social class and privilege of the boys, as well as their health and vitality. It is accompanied by popular music of the time, shown at the end of the scene to be coming from the radio that Meeks and Pitts have successfully constructed.

In the dormitory, Todd is attempting to write a poem while the others are engaged in outdoor recreation (again highlighting his more interior nature). Neil enters exuberantly and tells him about the auditions for a local production of *A Midsummer Night's Dream*. He jumps on the beds and says, 'For the first time in my whole life I know what I want to do. For the first time in my life, I'm going to do it, whether my father wants me to or not. *Carpe diem*!' (s.5).

Todd worries aloud about the logistics of Neil participating in the play without his father's permission. At first Neil brushes off Todd's objections, then becomes angry, saying, 'Jesus Todd, whose side are you on?' (s.5). In an attempt to change the subject, he asks Todd whether he will attend the upcoming meeting of the Dead Poets Society. Todd is reluctant and Neil accuses him of being unmoved by any of Mr Keating's teachings. Todd says, 'I'm not like you, all right? You say things and people listen.

I'm not like that' (s.5), implying they have different ways of processing Mr Keating's teaching. Neil attempts to cheer Todd out of his negative mood, snatching his poetry. Todd gives chase. Cameron enters the room and Neil grabs the book he is carrying and throws it to Todd; the three boys tease and chase each other around the room.

In an exterior scene, Knox is shown riding his bicycle down a steep hill, yelling exuberantly. He arrives at a rally where cheerleaders are giving the public school American-football team a noisy send-off as they board a bus. He spies Chris, in her cheerleading uniform, hugging her footballer boyfriend, Chet. This scene shows an important class contrast between the (still comparatively wealthy) public school with its 1950s Americana and the British-influenced upper-class environment of Welton Academy, and depicts the public-school students' more relaxed clothing and mannerisms and their opportunity for opposite-sex friendships and romantic relationships.

Key point

Neil and Knox are both seen, in this section, to be full of life, stirred up to passionate activity by Mr Keating's influence.

Q Is Mr Keating being cruel when he singles Todd out at the end of the lesson? Why or why not?

Section six: Chances

In the next scene, Mr Keating leads the boys outside. Each boy is required to read out a literary quotation before kicking a (soccer) football as hard as he can. Not all of them embrace the exercise, but Charlie in particular is shown to give an energetic performance.

The scene cuts to a school corridor where Neil is shouting that he got the part of Puck for which he had auditioned. He excitedly forges a letter of permission from his father while Todd looks on, seeming nervous on his friend's behalf.

The next scene shows a bagpiper piping in the dawn while Todd paces his room with pencil and paper. This implies that he has been up all night attempting to write his poem for class.

In the classroom, Knox reads out his poem about Chris while the other boys laugh surreptitiously. Mr Keating, however, encourages Knox, and Charlie pats him on the back when he sits down. Hopkins, another student, reads his composition, 'The cat sits on the mat' (s.6), demonstrating that Keating's teaching is not embraced by the entire class and is seen by some as a chance to slack off. Weir is careful to show a realistically varied response to Mr Keating.

When asked to read his poem, Todd says that he didn't complete the assignment. Mr Keating says, 'Mr Anderson thinks everything inside of him is worthless and embarrassing. Isn't that right, Todd? Isn't that your worst fear? Well, I think you're wrong. I think you have something inside of you that is worth a great deal' (s.6).

He then makes Todd stand up and demonstrate a 'barbaric yawp' (quoting from Walt Whitman), and asks Todd what the photo of Walt Whitman on the wall makes him think of; Todd, when pressed, says, 'a sweaty-toothed madman' (s.6). Mr Keating puts his hand over Todd's eyes and tells him to describe what he sees. Todd is soon carried away by his own momentum and composes a poem on the spot that impresses both Mr Keating and the class. As the class applauds, Mr Keating puts his hand on Todd's head in a fatherly gesture and says, 'Don't you forget this' (s.6).

The next scene is a soccer game outdoors, during which Beethoven's *Ode to Joy* plays. The boys are happy and lively and, at the end of the game, they lift Mr Keating (who has been enthusiastically refereeing from the sidelines) onto their shoulders. He appears delighted by their actions.

The boys are next seen in the cave, smoking pipes.

Key point

The boys are now comfortable in the cave, highlighting their transition from the interior to the exterior world.

Charlie plays the saxophone and recites his own composition ('Gotta do more, gotta be more' [s.6]).

Knox says, 'I can't take it any more, if I can't have Chris I'm going to kill myself' (s.6). He leaves the cave to phone Chris. The other boys go with him and cluster around the school payphone. To build up his courage, Knox says, '*Carpe diem*, even if it kills me' (s.6). In their brief phone conversation, Chris invites Knox to a party; he hangs up and triumphantly yells 'Yawp!', referencing Mr Keating's lesson.

Q Why does Mr Keating's approach to encouraging Todd work so well? How does Todd feel about Mr Keating at this point?

Section seven: Find your own walk

In the courtyard, Mr Keating asks Pitts, Cameron and Knox to walk around, to illustrate a point about conformity: each boy starts out at his own pace but they fall into a uniform stride very quickly. He explains his lesson, saying, 'We all have a great need for acceptance' (s.7). He then has all the boys walk around, asserting their own styles of walking, making for a strange sight as Mr Nolan peers out his window at the class. Charlie does not participate, asserting his 'right not to walk' (s. 7), which Mr Keating approves of, saying 'Thank you Mr Dalton, you just illustrated the point' (s. 7).

Key point

This is a notable scene as it highlights Mr Nolan's growing discomfort with Mr Keating's teaching methods.

That night, on the parapet of the school wall, Neil cheers up Todd, who has received the same birthday present from his parents as he did the previous year (a desk set). He makes a joke of it, saying the gift is aerodynamic and encourages Todd to throw it off the wall, which he does.

There is a cut to the cave, where the boys are reciting the Thoreau poem that opens the Dead Poets Society meetings, when they are surprised by Charlie arriving with two girls. After introducing the girls (Gloria and Tina) Charlie marks his face with Tina's lipstick, approximating his idea of a tribal marking, and announces that he now wants to be referred to as 'Nuwanda'.

Q What is the significance of Charlie changing his name?

Section eight: Unorthodox ideas

In the next scene, Knox arrives at the party Chris invited him to. He enthusiastically greets Chris, but she only asks whether he has brought anyone else then goes off to find Chet: clearly her invitation didn't have the romantic connotations Knox imagined. He aimlessly circulates, drinks whisky offered to him and eventually ends up on a couch with Chris, who is sleeping. He says, '*carpe diem*' (s.8) and kisses her on the forehead. Others point this out to her boyfriend, Chet, who attacks Knox. Chris, now awake, shows concern for Knox and he apologises to her. This scene cuts back and forth between Knox at the party and the other boys with Tina and Gloria in the cave; this is the point where the boys are attempting romantic encounters with girls, inspired by Mr Keating's earlier assertion that the point of poetry is to woo women.

Back in the cave, Charlie reveals he has published an article demanding that girls be admitted to Welton in the school paper, in the name of the Dead Poets Society. The other boys are dismayed at this public exposure of the society's existence, but Charlie defends himself, saying that the spirit of the Dead Poets Society involves more than simply reading poetry.

The next scene is in the chapel, where grim-faced members of the administration admonish the students for the Dead Poets Society article that Charlie wrote. As Mr Nolan demands that the guilty party come forward, a telephone rings somewhere in the audience. Charlie stands up, holding the phone and says it is God calling Mr Nolan, 'He says we should have girls at Welton' (s.8).

In Mr Nolan's office, the headmaster tells Charlie he knows that the boy is deliberately trying to be expelled. He administers corporal punishment, beating Charlie with a heavy wooden paddle and inflicting significant pain. When Charlie emerges, the boys are waiting, worried. They ask what happened and Charlie tells them he is supposed to turn everyone in and apologise to the school. When Neil asks, 'What are you going to do, Charlie?' he smiles and says, 'The name is Nuwanda' (s.8), implying his rebellious spirit is not broken.

In the next scene, Mr Nolan confronts Mr Keating about his unorthodox teaching methods – although not yet accusing him of influencing the boys negatively. Mr Keating says, 'I always thought the idea of education was to learn to think for yourself'. Mr Nolan replies, 'At these boys' age? Not on your life. Tradition, John, discipline. Prepare them for college and the rest will take care of itself' (s.8).

In the common room, Charlie is recounting his beating from Mr Nolan. Mr Keating arrives and advises caution, explaining that the boys may have misinterpreted his philosophies, saying, 'There's a time for daring and there's a time for caution and a wise man understands which is called for' (s.8). He tempers this speech by joking with the boys and, despite the reprimand, they seem quite happy after his visit.

Next, Neil rides his bicycle to rehearsals at Henley Hall and is seen smiling at the scene that greets him on stage. When he returns to school, the boys are running to the dining room as the bell rings but he goes to his room, where he finds his father waiting. Mr Perry doesn't allow Neil to explain and immediately orders him to quit the play. He says, 'Who put you up to it? Was it this new man, this Mr Keating?' (s.8) but Neil defends his teacher, claiming he had nothing to do with it.

Key point

Mr Perry says, 'I don't care if the world comes to an end tomorrow night, you are through with that play' (s.8), which is a case of dramatic irony since, for Neil, the world does in fact come to an end the following night. He also says, 'I made a great many sacrifices to get you here, Neil, and you will not let me down'.

Q By publishing the article in the school newspaper, does Charlie betray the Dead Poets Society?

Section nine: Neil's dream

Neil immediately goes to Mr Keating's room for advice. He asks about the photograph on the desk of a woman who, it is implied, is Keating's wife or girlfriend, who is still in London.

When Neil explains his situation. Mr Keating advises him to tell his father how passionate he is about acting. When Neil protests, Mr Keating says, 'You're acting for him too, you're playing the part of the dutiful son' (s.9). When Mr Keating presses him, Neil says 'Isn't there an easier way?' When Keating says no, Neil says, 'I'm trapped' but the teacher says, 'No you're not' (s.9). Neil also explains that his family is not of the same social and economic class as many of the other boys', implying that his parents have much more to lose if he is not successful at Welton. He says, 'We're not a rich family like Charlie's' (s. 9).

In the morning, Knox goes to Chris' high school and reads a poem to her in her classroom, embarrassing her but showing his commitment to the ideals of the Dead Poets Society. Back at Welton, the boys surround Knox for details, impressed by his courage.

In the classroom, Mr Keating and Neil are alone. The boy lies to his teacher, saying his father has given permission for him to be in the play. Mr Keating seems to suspect that Neil was not able to get up the courage to actually speak to his father and appears worried.

As the boys get ready to go to the performance of *A Midsummer Night's Dream*, Chris arrives to confront Knox about his behaviour, which has embarrassed her. By the end of their conversation, Knox has persuaded her to accompany him to the play as his date.

Towards the end of the performance, Mr Perry enters and stands at the back of the room. Neil notices his father just before delivering his closing monologue, giving the speech a double meaning (with lines such as, 'if we shadows have offended ... do not reprimand', s.9), as he is also directly addressing his father and asking for forgiveness. The play is a success, receiving a standing ovation, particularly for Neil as Puck.

After yelling at Mr Keating – 'You stay away from my son!' (s.9) – when he tries to congratulate Neil, Mr Perry hustles his son out through the celebrating crowd.

At home, Neil sits with his parents. He looks beseechingly at his mother, but she is, like Neil, unwilling to stand up to his father. Mr Perry informs Neil he is withdrawing him from Welton the following day and enrolling him in a military school program. Mr Perry attempts to use guilt to manipulate Neil again, saying, 'You have opportunities that I never even dreamt of' (s.9). Neil says, 'I've got to tell you what I feel!' Mr Perry cuts him off, saying, 'Tell me what you feel. What is it? Is it more of this, this acting business? Because you can forget that'. Neil pauses for a long time but is unable to bring himself to confront his father, and finally says, 'Nothing'. Mr Perry leaves the room and Mrs Perry kneels behind Neil, who speaks his final words: 'I was good. I was really good' (s.9).

In their bedroom, while Mrs Perry cries in bed her husband says, 'It's going to be all right' (s.9).

Neil strips to his long johns, opens the windows and stands looking out at the snow, with Puck's crown of branches on his head. This symbolises his final embracing of the natural, wild, Romantic world, and his inability to live the restricted life his father is dictating.

He goes downstairs to his father's study and shoots himself with his father's gun. Mr Perry hears the shot, finds that Neil's room is empty then goes downstairs to investigate. Opening the study door, he smells the gunpowder then finds Neil dead behind the desk. He cries out mournfully, 'my son, my poor son!'; Mrs Perry screams hysterically, 'He's all right, he's all right!' (s.9).

At Welton, the boys wake Todd. Charlie tells him Neil is dead. They all go outside in the snow, where Todd throws up. He says, 'He wouldn't have done it, it was his father. He wouldn't have left us ... his father did it, his father killed him' (s.9), then runs towards the water.

In an empty classroom, Mr Keating looks at the textbook inscribed with the Dead Poets Society rules and sobs silently at Neil's desk, showing genuine grief.

The next scene is Neil's funeral in the chapel, at which Mr Nolan claims he will, at the request of Neil's parents, conduct a thorough inquiry into their son's death.

Key point

His request for an inquiry tell us that Neil's father is not willing to accept any responsibility for his son's death.

In the dormitory, the boys are nervous because Cameron hasn't shown up for their meeting. He finally does and admits he has spoken to the administration and supported its claim that Mr Keating is responsible for Neil's death. He says, 'Believe what you want, I say let Keating fry ... you can't save Keating but you can save yourselves' (s.9).

Mr Nolan pressures the boys one by one, in front of their parents, into signing a document asserting that Mr Keating is responsible for Neil's death – with the exception of Charlie who punches Cameron in his fury at the injustice and is then expelled. Todd protests and says to Cameron '[It's] not true, Cameron, you know that' (s.9) and to Mr Nolan, 'What's gonna to happen to Mr Keating?' (s.9), but he too signs the condemnatory document in the end – the last boy to do so.

Key point

The fact that Todd speaks up, even ineffectually, at a time where there is so much on the line shows how much he has changed as a character.

Mr McAllister is seen walking outside in the snow with his class, teaching them Latin vocabulary. He looks up at the window where Mr Keating is standing and waves to him. He is the only staff member to show Mr Keating any sympathy or friendliness.

Q Why is it important that Todd is the last person to sign the document?

Section ten: 'O Captain! my Captain'

In Mr Keating's classroom, Mr Nolan takes over the class. When asked where the class is up to in the poetry textbook, Cameron says, 'We skipped around a lot sir, we covered the Romantics and some of the chapters on post Civil War literature' (s.10). When Mr Nolan asks about the Realists, Cameron says they also 'skipped most of that' (s.10), showing that Mr Keating focused both philosophically and thematically on the Romantic Movement. So Mr Nolan announces they will start from the beginning.

Mr Keating arrives to collect his personal effects from his office adjoining the classroom. Mr Nolan asks Cameron to read from Dr

Pritchard's essay on understanding poetry and, on hearing that it has been ripped out of every book, gives Cameron his own copy. The boy reads aloud the staid and passionless instructions for analysing poetry that Mr Keating had derided. Mr Keating, visible in the side room, catches Todd's eye; as he walks through the classroom on his way out, Todd stands up suddenly and tells him the boys were forced to sign the document that incriminated him. When Mr Nolan reprimands him, Todd responds, 'But it wasn't his fault' (s.10), asserting himself even to the school's highest authority figure. Mr Nolan threatens expulsion for anyone else who speaks out of turn, and orders Mr Keating to leave. As Keating reaches the door, Todd climbs up on his desk, as Mr Keating had in the earlier class, and exclaims, 'O Captain! my Captain' (s.10). Amidst Mr Nolan's protests, Knox, Pitts and Meeks follow his lead, as do several other boys, including Hopkins, who was previously resistant to Mr Keating's teaching. Keating smiles as half the class is shown standing on their desks. He says, 'Thank you boys, thank you' (s.10), the final line of the film.

Key point

The final shot is of Todd's face, to show that Mr Keating has had a positive influence on at least one life.

Q Why is it important to show that not all the boys stand up on their desks for Mr Keating? What point is Weir making with this choice?

CHARACTERS & RELATIONSHIPS

Mr Keating and Neil

Key quotes

> You're acting for him too. You're playing the part of the dutiful son. (s.9; Mr Keating to Neil)
>
> Isn't there an easier way? (s.9; Neil to Mr Keating)

John Keating is the most influential character in the film. He is not, however, the main character in a traditional sense. The role of protagonist is shared between Neil and Todd. Mr Keating instead acts as a catalyst for the emotional journeys on which the boys (Neil and Todd in particular) embark.

Unlike the other teachers at the school, John Keating was once a student at Welton Academy himself. This implies he comes from a privileged background but chose to become a teacher rather than following a more lucrative path. He has taught abroad prior to joining the Welton staff, and even returns to Welton although his wife or girlfriend (it is not clear which) has stayed behind in England. He brings with him a modern sensibility and optimistic expectations for the boys he teaches. He feels that his students are intelligent and creative and could have a lot to say if they are given the opportunity. This opinion contrasts with the views of other teachers, even kindly ones like Mr McAllister, who feel that boys of this age need strong guidance, discipline and boundaries in order to succeed.

Mr Keating undergoes an emotional journey in the film. He encourages the boys to follow their dreams, to connect emotionally with literature and to stand up for what they believe in. However, it comes as a shock to him when Neil, who has been forbidden to choose his own path by his parents, commits suicide. This act shakes his worldview, which dictates that boys needed freedom and encouragement more than anything else in order to succeed. However, the final scene in which the boys bravely stand up and give tribute to Mr Keating seems to go some way towards renewing his faith. Indeed, Neil's ability to make the choice to kill himself can be seen as a test of Keating's philosophy that boys should be allowed to control their own fates. If he truly believes that his students have the right to choose their own paths, then he must, painful as it is, believe that Neil had the right to choose to kill himself.

Key points

His tenure at Welton is a significant and practical test of Mr Keating's beliefs, which have, as far as the viewer can know, been merely theoretical and somewhat idealistic up until this point.

Mr Keating believes that the students experience life as poignantly and deeply as grown men, and with Neil's death he is proven correct in an unexpected way.

Mr Keating and Todd

Key quotes

> Mr Anderson thinks that everything inside of him is worthless and embarrassing. Isn't that right, Todd? Isn't that your worst fear? Well, I think you're wrong. I think you have something inside of you that is worth a great deal. (s.6; Mr Keating to Todd)

Mr Keating pays special attention to Todd from the beginning. He notices that the boy is uncomfortable and shy and so at first avoids forcing him to speak in class. Once Todd becomes marginally more comfortable (though still extremely shy), Mr Keating challenges him and pushes him to explore his inner poetic potential.

Todd, for his part, is immediately influenced by Mr Keating though he gives no outward sign of this. He is seen alone in his room writing 'Seize the day!' and he is also shown working on his poem for class at dawn, implying he has stayed up all night long.

Todd is serious and places high value on justice and accuracy; he is less willing than the other boys to deviate from the original values of the Dead Poets Society, and even expresses his unwillingness to join if it means breaking the rule that all members must read.

Key points

Todd and Mr Keating have one of the most important relationships in the film. While Todd is a quiet character and does not receive as much screen time as Neil, he is in fact, from a literary standpoint, the narrator of the film.

Mr Keating wants to inspire all the boys, but he sees special potential in Todd, even before Todd demonstrates his poetic ability. This implies that Mr Keating is somehow able to perceive exceptional ability instinctively, casting him as a mentor in the tradition of a wizard or priest.

Mr Keating and the Welton Academy staff

Key quotes

I always thought the idea of education was to learn to think for yourself. (s.8) (Mr Keating to Mr Nolan)

Not a cynic, a realist. (s.3; Mr McAllister describing himself to Mr Keating)

Mr Keating clashes with Mr Nolan and Mr McAllister over the type of education that is best for young men. McAllister, for instance, is obviously fond of his students but feels rote learning is needed to suppress the boys' tendency to be unfocused. He is wounded when Keating implies he is a cynic, stating that he is in fact a realist. It is clear that McAllister considers Keating to be somewhat naïve in his teaching philosophy, but still respects him; even when Mr Keating is utterly disgraced, Mr McAllister is seen waving to him (s.9).

Mr Nolan, on the other hand, views Mr Keating's endangerment of the school's reputation as unforgivable. The two men do have an initial civilised discussion addressing the former's reservations about the latter's teaching methods, in which Mr Nolan attempts to relate to Mr Keating as one teacher to another, mentioning how hard he found it to give up teaching when he moved to the position of headmaster (s. 8). Mr Keating for his part, while respectful, says he finds it hard to picture Mr Nolan as a teacher, implying he feels that the headmaster lacks the patience and understanding necessary to be an effective teacher. Keating appears unafraid of reprimand throughout his tenure at Welton, implying that either his livelihood does not depend upon his job or that he is willing to put his livelihood at risk for his ideals.

Mr Nolan is entirely willing to blame Mr Keating for Neil's death and he exerts an enormous amount of pressure to ensure that the boys (at least officially) do the same. It is not explored whether Mr Nolan believes this to be an accurate assessment of the situation or whether he simply gives priority to the good of the school above all else. Both men are present in the final scene, and Mr Nolan shouts at the boys to sit down when they stand on their desks, suggesting that he is unforgiving and, in the final moments, still firm in his belief that Mr Keating's teaching methods are dangerous and negative.

Key points

Mr Keating and the other teachers are each convinced that his own philosophy of teaching is the most effective and important, despite the inherent conflict of their views.

The debate is represented as either realism vs cynicism (for viewers who agree with Mr Keating) or realism vs idealism (for viewers who agree with Mr McAllister or Mr Nolan). All the masters believe they are acting as realists and that they are being responsible and helpful to their students.

Neil and Todd

Key quotes

Jesus Todd, whose side are you on? (s.5; Neil to Todd)

I'm not like you, all right? You say things and people listen. I'm not like that. (s.5; Todd to Neil)

Neil, you're crazy. (s.5; Todd to Neil)

Todd's main role is as an observer of the more externally dynamic character, Neil. In this sense, he is similar to Nick Carraway, the narrator of F Scott Fitzgerald's iconic novel, *The Great Gatsby*. Carraway is the character who, at the end of the novel, learns from what has happened, while Jay Gatsby, the titular character, follows his emotions and ends up dying. Clear comparisons to Todd and Neil can be drawn.

Neil is kind to Todd from the beginning, offering him friendship and inclusion in his social group. He encourages Todd when the latter is shy and afraid of judgement, and allows him to join the Dead Poets Society without the supposed requirement of having to read aloud. Neil certainly sees much of himself in his friend – Todd's behaviour towards authority figures (and indeed towards most people) is reminiscent of Neil's subservience to his father. While Todd's rebellion and hope for the future remain mainly internal, Neil moves beyond that to open defiance of his father. Neil is both an inspiration and a warning to Todd. He represents the twin dangers that Todd faces: following his passions too fervently and repressing his own desires too much, resulting in the same kind of desperation that Neil faces. Neil is unable to achieve balance, but the film closes with the implication that Todd will fare better.

Key points

Todd and Neil are similar in many ways, yet Neil is more active and determined. Normally these would be positive qualities, but because they are unchecked they bring about Neil's downfall.

Todd and Neil are the characters whose internal journeys are followed most clearly by the film, and they are also the characters upon whom Mr Keating has the strongest influence.

Neil and his father, Mr Perry

Key quotes

Oh, he won't disappoint us. (s.1; Mr Perry to Mr Nolan)

Tell me what you feel. (s.9; Mr Perry to Neil)

You have opportunities that I never even dreamt of. (s.9; Mr Perry to Neil)

Neil is submissive towards his father prior to its formation, but through the Dead Poets Society he gains the fortitude to rebel. His father is never shown hitting him; rather, he uses guilt as a weapon, reminding Neil of how much his success means to his mother (s.1) and how much his parents have sacrificed in order for him to attend Welton (s.8). This guilt, presumably meant to make Neil feel gratitude and respect, instead has the effect of smothering him. Anything he enjoys, even harmless and academically-oriented activities like sub-editing the school yearbook, is forbidden by his father, revealing that Mr Perry has an unrealistic approach to parenting and expects Neil to refrain from emotional or social involvement in activities unless there is a direct practical benefit. Whether Mr Perry is essentially well-meaning is a significant point of debate for viewers of the film. He is not a sympathetic character, but Kurtwood Smith, the actor portraying him, mentioned in an interview on the DVD commentary his personal desire that the character be 'understandable' without being excused by the audience.

Neil is put in impossible situations by his father's approach to parenting, e.g. when his father confronts him about his extra-curricular activities in front of the other boys (s.1). When Neil protests, Mr Perry furiously reprimands him for defying his father in front of others, despite the fact that it was Mr Perry who chose to start the conversation in the presence of the other boys. This sort of treatment leaves Neil feeling powerless and without options, as whatever he does tends to lead to conflict with his father. He is a superior student and earns straight A grades in all of his classes, either because of his own academic enthusiasm, because he feels pressured to do so by his father or by some combination of factors. It is likely that Neil's college applications would actually have been enriched by the extra-curricular involvement he so desires, which reveals his father's lack of true understanding. Mr Perry's frustration may, in fact, stem partly from his imperfect understanding of the best way to promote Neil to a higher social class. Indeed, his chosen profession for Neil (medicine) is extremely stereotypical, suggesting he has only vague notions of how Neil could achieve the social and economic success on which Mr Perry is so intent.

It is essential to note that Mr Perry does, finally, ask Neil what he wants, saying, 'Tell me what you feel' (s.9). He does this in a confrontational and dismissive way, but he does ask and pause for an answer. This is Neil's crucial opportunity to engage with his father and explain his passion for acting. However, the history of their relationship and the submission that has become ingrained in Neil throughout his upbringing overwhelm him and, despite Mr Keating explicitly urging him to tell his father about his aspirations, Neil is silent. This is his one great failure in the film. His suicide can be seen as a response to the intense pressure his father has put on him, but it can also be seen as a response to his personal failing to truly live up to the ideals of the Dead Poets Society, which he has, up until this confrontation, embraced so passionately.

Key points

Neil and his father suffer differences of both generation and class; while Mr Perry would have spent his adolescent years in a middle- (or possible working-) class environment, at Welton Neil is surrounded by boys whose goals go beyond economic security (which, for many of them, would be a certainty). By sending Neil to Welton, Mr Perry may have inadvertently increased the gap between his and his son's worldviews.

The relationship between Neil and his father is pivotal and open to interpretation by the viewer. This openness is a constant choice on Weir's part and elevates the film to a complex emotional narrative rather than a simple villain-and-victim story. Neil's own actions must be considered in the context of analysing his relationship with his father.

Knox Overstreet and Chris Noel

Key quotes

If I don't have Chris, I'm going to kill myself. (s.6; Knox to the boys)

I've been calm all my life, I'm going to do something about that. (s.6; Knox to the boys)

Knox exercises the ideals of the Dead Poets Society in a way that none of the other boys does. Mr Keating claims that poetry is written primarily to woo women (s.5) and Knox takes this to its logical conclusion, not only reading poetry to Chris at her school but also writing an original piece for her.

The relationship between Knox and Chris is chaste and idealistic; they are barely acquainted but are mutually enthralled by one another. When Knox kisses Chris at the party, he kisses her forehead, showing that his interest is romantic and not primarily sexual. This is in keeping with the literary atmosphere of the film. The concept of courtly love in Renaissance poetry is referenced in Knox's actions, with chaste adoration taking priority over sexual fulfilment. If Neil takes passion from the Dead Poets Society and Neil takes courage, Knox takes idealism. When he is building up the courage to call Chris, he says '*Carpe diem*, even if it kills me' (s.6).

Key points

Knox's relationship with Chris illustrates the innocent and idealistic interpretation of Mr Keating's teachings.

The presence of Chris is important to make the Dead Poets Society more than simply theoretical in its influence (apart from Neil's suicide). By taking the ideals of the Dead Poets Society and putting them into practice, Knox proves Mr Keating right about the relevance of poetry to everyday life.

Minor Characters

Steven Meeks and the other boys

Key quotes

Nothing they didn't already know. (s.9; Meeks to Todd, who asked what he told Mr Nolan during the inquiry)

Relationship

Meeks is bright and well-liked by the other boys. Like Pitts, he takes Mr Keating's teasing with good humour. He stands on his desk in the final scene, although he is not among the first few to do so.

Gerard Pitts and the other boys

Key quotes

> I might be going to Yale. But I might not be. (s.8; Pitts to Gloria and Tina in the cave)

Relationship

Pitts is an affable character who is often paired with Meeks. He is patient when Mr Keating makes jokes about his name and is among the first of the boys to follow Todd in standing on his desk in the final scene.

Richard Cameron and the other boys

Key quotes

> If you guys are smart, you'll do exactly what I did and cooperate. (s.9; Cameron to the other boys)

Relationship

Cameron's role is pivotal, as it is his willingness to cooperate with the Welton administration that exerts pressure on the other boys to do the same. If the boys had been able to close ranks and uniformly deny Mr Keating's responsibility for Neil's death, it is possible that the administration would have failed to justify firing Mr Keating; it is unlikely that they would have expelled all six remaining members of the Dead Poets Society.

Cameron is interested in Mr Keating's teachings, but it is clear he doesn't embrace them on an emotional level. He claims to be dedicated to the school's honour code (s.9); whether this is his true motivation is unclear. In the final scene, while reading from the poetry textbook (s.10), Cameron's voice drops when he sees Mr Keating and he clearly feels some measure of shame about his actions. However, he is able to continue reading, and refuses to stand on his desk along with the others.

Mr McAllister and Mr Keating

Key quotes

Not a cynic, a realist. (s.3; Mr McAllister, about himself, to Mr Keating)

Relationship

Mr McAllister, who teaches Latin at Welton, disagrees with John Keating's teaching methods, but he does so because he is worried about the best interest of the boys. He also appears to respect Mr Keating's right to choose his own teaching philosophy even if they disagree; he doesn't interfere with the class even during the scene where the boys are ripping their textbooks apart at Mr Keating's urging (s.3). McAllister worries that Keating is encouraging impossible and unrealistic dreams in the boys that will only lead to bitter disappointment. Their disagreement about what is best for the students represents a main tension in the film. Towards the end of the film (s.9), when Keating has been fired, McAllister shows kindness by waving to him, despite this certainly being disapproved of by Mr Nolan. Importantly, this occurs when McAllister has taken his students outside to learn Latin by naming things within the school grounds, showing he has adopted some of Keating's tamer teaching techniques himself, to some extent unifying the two opposing schools of thought. Mr Keating smiles when he sees this.

THEMES, IDEAS & VALUES

Conformity and identity

Key quotes

'What good amid [foolishness and faithlessness], o me, o life?' Answer: that you are here. That life exists, and identity. (s.3; Mr Keating to his class)

I've been calm all my life. I'm going to do something about that. (s.6; Knox to the other boys)

Now, we all have a great need for acceptance. But you must trust that your beliefs are unique, your own, even though others may think them odd or unpopular. (s.7; Mr Keating to his class)

I always thought the idea of education was to learn to think for yourself. (s.8; Mr Keating to Mr Nolan)

Welton Academy is an extremely strict environment for students, insisting on conformity in behaviour and appearance. The motivation for this is to produce graduates who will be able to conform and perform in competitive professional fields. Some students deal with the pressure to conform better than others, depending on their individual nature and the amount of pressure they are under.

The Dead Poets Society offers the boys who join a chance to highlight their individual feelings and experiences, rather than being subsumed into the crowd. There are two texts included in the film that highlight this theme most clearly. One is the quotation from Thoreau's *Walden* that is read by Neil at the opening of the Dead Poets Society meetings: 'I wanted to live deep and suck out all the marrow of life ... and not, when I had come to die, discover that I had not lived' (s.4). The other is from Robert Frost's poem, 'The Road not Taken': 'Two roads diverged in a wood and I, I took the one less travelled by, and that has made all the difference' (s.7), quoted by Mr Keating. Both encourage the boys to assert their individuality, but it is notable that the text Neil reads focuses more on spontaneity and self-gratification, while the Frost poem quoted by Mr Keating uses phrases that point more towards exploration and healthy curiosity. These texts represent two approaches to individuality: the impulsive and the exploratory. In this sense, they represent the two paths which Neil and Todd choose to follow, respectively, when they find and assert their individual desires and voices.

The other two characters who are shown asserting their individuality are Knox and Charlie. They mirror Todd and Neil in their approaches. Knox manages to use the ideals of the Dead Poets Society to motivate himself to woo Chris, the girl in whom he is romantically interested, while Charlie is driven to risky stunts and eventually is expelled for his impetuous and rash behaviour.

Mr Keating is also seen to assert individuality. He dresses and behaves differently from his colleagues, from his first appearance to his last. He is comfortable with his own methods and beliefs, and he is willing and able to defend his choices to Mr McAllister and Mr Nolan when confronted about his teaching methods. However, the school's treatment of him as a scapegoat also highlights the costs and risks of individuality and nonconformity; when a crisis arises, the person who is unique, most individual and visible, is targeted as a bad influence.

Mr Keating demonstrates that individuality has both benefits and risks. While Todd and Knox benefit from their assertion of individuality, become more fulfilled and happier, Neil and Charlie's individualism has negative consequences for them and their families. Only Mr Keating, as the adult character, is shown to have discovered both the dark and positive sides of self-awareness: not only the self-fulfilment but also the social and emotional costs.

The most notable demonstration of self-determination and individuality in the film is Neil's decision to kill himself. While there are many factors at play that contribute to his emotional state prior to his suicide (notably the teachings of Mr Keating and the pressures exerted by Neil's parents and the school), his own role and actions in his death must not be ignored. It may not be entirely informed or rational, but he makes an independent decision, which results in an explosive example of the kind of individualism that is mainly demonstrated in a theoretical and interior manner in the film. Neil's decision shows that individualism is, in its most extreme application, the ability to control one's own life and, by extension, death.

Key points

In such a highly restricted setting, small rebellions become key to establishing an individual identity.

Individuality is shown to offer greater potential for fulfilment and self-actualisation, in the cases of Mr Keating, Todd and Knox, but it is also shown to have risks, in the cases of Mr Keating, Neil and Charlie.

Individualism is, at its core, the ability to determine one's own fate.

Q Is the pressure on the boys at Welton a good or bad thing? In what ways might it be both?

Q Why do the boys react differently to the pressure to conform?

Q What does Welton stand to lose by embracing new methods of thinking and teaching? Why would the administration be resistant to change?

Expectations and appearances

Key quotes

Neil, we expect great things from you this year. (s.1; Mr Nolan to Neil)

I'm sorry, I didn't know you were here. (s.3; Mr McAllister to Mr Keating in his classroom)

You have but slumbered here while these visions did appear. (s.9; Neil, as Puck in *A Midsummer's Night Dream*)

The characters in *Dead Poets Society* are often motivated by their expectations of one another. The students expect their teachers to perform in a certain way, and when Mr Keating flouts that expectation reactions vary from fear to delight. Parental expectations are important to the film, not only in the sense that parents expect the boys to be high achievers, but also in that their expectations of the boys' behaviour are inflexible and unable to adapt to changing circumstances, as is seen when Neil's father is genuinely surprised about his son's decision to take his own life.

Appearance is often taken at face value in the film. The Welton staff values neatness and uniformity, as well as natural beauty. It is not a simple dichotomy in which the traditional Welton staff are cruel and unfeeling while Mr Keating is sympathetic and passionate; instead the contrast is made between Mr Keating being eager to look beyond appearances while the rest of the staff believe appearances give an accurate, full picture of a situation. If a boy looks neat and happy, the staff infer that he is. If a campus is beautiful and serene in appearance (as Welton is shown to be, in many lingering shots), then it is presumed to be beautiful and serene in its atmosphere and practice. Mr Keating, on the other hand, examines appearances and looks beyond them to discover what is hidden. This is illustrated in his treatment of Todd, who seems to be a poor, nervous student but in fact has deep reserves of passion and literary intuition.

However, Mr Keating's assessments are not always accurate. Like Mr Perry, he is genuinely surprised by Neil's suicide. It is suggested that he knows Neil is lying to him about gaining his father's permission to perform in the play, but he does not pursue the matter because he has faith that his pupil will act rationally and bravely – that he will act like a grown man rather than an adolescent. He fails to understand how sensitive Neil is, and assumes that encouragement is all that is needed to shore up the boy's confidence. His expectation of Neil is an overestimation and, as a result, he experiences significant pain when told of his suicide. While Neil's decision is his own, Mr Keating undoubtedly feels some measure of responsibility for his failure in an area in which he is often so talented: understanding the inner lives of his students.

Key points

Appearances are often taken at face value in the film, with much of the narrative action occurring internally, particularly in the case of Todd.

Neil is very expressive and seems to make his feelings clear to those around him but, upon his death, it becomes clear that no one really understands him, as his final actions are a shock to all who know him, shattering their expectations of him.

Q Why does Mr Keating understand Todd so well?

Q What other expectations, besides those of appearances, are challenged in the film?

Q Mr Keating's faith in the boys could be seen as idealistic. Is he an idealist? Is the rest of the staff cynical? Which characters might be seen as realists in their outlook?

The natural vs the civilised

Key quotes

This is it ... it's my cave. (s.7; Charlie to Gloria and Tina)

You see we'd gather at the old Indian cave and take turns reading from Thoreau, Whitman, Shelley. The biggies. (s.3; Mr Keating describing the Dead Poets Society)

[The cave] is beyond the stream. I know where it is. (s.3; Neil to the other boys)

It's starting to sound dangerous. (s.3; Cameron, looking at the map to the cave)

One of the most significant points of the film is the first foray by the boys into the school grounds at night, where they reconvene the Dead Poets Society. This is done in a setting that is the complete opposite of the ordered and civilised school building: a rough and natural cave in the woods. This point marks the beginning of Neil's transformation from rational to Romantic or instinctual – or, to put it another way, his transformation from civilised to natural. While this transformation is not necessarily to blame for his suicide, the process does lead to the events that precipitate it. In the suicide scene, the theme of the natural is continued with the crown of twigs Neil wears before he shoots himself. He also takes particular care to open the windows and stand in front of them for a moment without his shirt on, signifying a moment in which his own natural body experiences the natural world. Similarly, upon learning of Neil's death, Todd immediately runs outdoors into nature, as an instinctual reaction to his grief. He continues towards the lake (the natural world) and away from the school buildings (the constructed world), unable to remain confined indoors at the height of his emotional pain. Weir highlights the physical world visually, showing the progression of seasons as a metaphor for the process of the characters. From the richness of the harvest season, when the film opens, to the death in winter, the timeline reflects the narrative action. Most notably, the film closes in the winter, which is when Neil's death occurs, but it is also a season of rest, when animals hibernate and plants begin the process of regeneration. Thematically, this implies that a period of healing will follow for the boys and Mr Keating, after the pain of Neil's death.

The adult characters are generally presented as having allegiance to one side of the philosophical spectrum or the other, either the natural and self-focused or the civilised and group-focused. Mr Keating represents the head of the natural faction and Mr Nolan represents the civilised. Each proponent believes his own school of thought to have the more positive effects – Nolan values success, achievement and security, while Keating values happiness, fulfilment and self-awareness. Both believe they are doing the right thing for the boys in their care. Mr McAllister is at first aligned with Mr Nolan but near the film's end takes his students outside, demonstrating that he is able to take on board some of Mr Keating's methods and apply them to his own teaching. None of the adult characters set out to deliberately victimise the students; all believe that their motives are positive, so who the villain of the film is (if there is one) is open to interpretation. Even Mr Perry seems to be (while misguided) motivated at least partly by a desire to see Neil achieve the kind of security that, he believes, brings happiness.

The only truly villainous act, in this context, is to refuse to pick either side and instead to switch allegiance back and forth, for self-serving reasons. Neil states this openly when he takes issue with Todd's apparent lack of emotional reaction to the Dead Poets Society, saying, 'You're in the club. Being in the club means being stirred up by things' (s.5). When Todd asks whether Neil, in that case, wants him out, Neil replies, 'I want you in! But being in means you gotta do something, not just say you're in' (s.5). Of course, Todd is indeed stirred up, but his reaction is highly internalised compared to Neil's. This exchange highlights the importance, to the boys, of being loyal to one side of the philosophical debate or the other. Todd's guilt in the final scene arises from feeling that he himself has proved to be a traitor to Mr Keating's side of the conflict, by signing the document blaming his teacher for Neil's suicide.

Cameron, by being the first to point the finger at Mr Keating in order to avoid taking any measure of blame himself, betrays the group in the worst possible way. While the boys are examining a map to work out how to reach the Dead Poets Society cave, he notably says, 'It's starting to sound dangerous' (s.3), which displays his reluctance to leave the ordered world of the school for the wild world of the forest and the cave.

By contrast, Neil is the only student who is already familiar with the cave when Mr Keating first mentions it, implying that he has been exploring around the grounds on his own. This highlights his affinity for and attraction to the natural world and its values of freedom and self-sufficiency. He leads the boys to the cave, both literally and metaphorically; he is the character upon whom the natural world exerts the strongest pull.

The film does not necessarily seek to promote one view as better than the other, but rather to examine the difficulties that arise when they come into conflict, both internally and externally.

Key points

The woods (both within the school grounds and in the play) represent the natural, instinctual, emotional world that becomes all-consuming for Neil.

The fact that Mr McAllister is able to combine the views of Mr Nolan and Mr Keating is important and implies that change, in a less extreme and more palatable way, may come to Welton after all because of Mr Keating's discussions with Mr McAllister.

Q How does the play in which Neil performs (Shakespeare's *A Midsummer Night's Dream*) relate to this theme?

Q What other images of the natural world in the film support this theme?

Q Are nature and civilisation always opposed? In what ways might they be complementary?

The value of youth and the inevitability of death

Key quotes

Believe it or not, each and every once of us in this room is one day going to stop breathing, turn cold and die. (s.2; Mr Keating to his class)

Neil's dead. (s.9; Charlie to Todd)

He wouldn't have done it ... he wouldn't have left us. (s.9; Todd to the other boys, regarding Neil's suicide)

Welton Academy can be seen as a source of ever-renewing youth. Boys attend the school, graduate and are replaced by new boys. But, on an individual level, youth is in fact quickly spent and precious. Mr Keating encourages the boys to live their lives fully because someday they will all die, a thought that is generally only a distant reality for most young people. Mr Keating encourages the boys to face their own mortality and, rather than being afraid, to use that as a motivation to achieve. This is a very different approach from that of their parents, who also encourage the boys to achieve but with very different methods and motivations: their message is that youth is a time to establish oneself and that life can be enjoyed later. This idea of delayed gratification is the opposite of Mr Keating's mantra to 'seize the day' and to make each moment as fulfilling as possible.

Weir highlights the healthy vitality of the boys in multiple scenes of soccer, fencing, rowing, bicycling and similar activities. Only one boy, a minor character, is ever shown to be ill or infirm (the other boys tease him and call him 'Spaz'). In this way, Weir constructs an illusion of an atmosphere of invincible youthfulness, which is shattered by Neil's suicide. This illusion was important to American society as a whole in the era in which the film was set; the boys would have been born during World War II and, while it is unlikely that many of their fathers fought in the conflict (given their implied social class they may have served as non-combative officers, or more likely been excluded from conscription via educational exclusions), many of their contemporaries would have. The *Dead Poets Society* students belong to the first generation to grow up in America after the Allied victory in the war and their youthful vitality and hope for the future symbolise the health of the US as a whole. Even more was invested in the contemporary youth of the country as they represented a victorious American future under the ongoing threat of the Cold War, which was well under way by 1959, the year in which the film is set. Neil's death could be symbolically interpreted as the death of the American dream; his father is a self-made man in a capitalist society who, through hard work, has propelled his son into the upper echelons of society, and Mr Keating's seemingly anti-capitalist thinking (his philosophy prioritises fulfilment over achievement) is blamed for Neil's death. This interpretation makes sense, considering that the reaction of the school administration implies there is much more at stake than the life of a single student and that Neil's death represents something sinister afoot at Welton. The idea of young men dying without need would have been unthinkable and unacceptable to Neil's parents' generation, who had seen thousands of young American men die in the war. The 1950s were supposed to be a peaceful and prosperous time in America and Neil's death challenges that idea. In this sense, Welton is a microcosm of the US. Like the country itself, Welton espouses the ideals of a meritocracy and the principle that hard work is rewarded by success, while at the same time enforcing a class system that is a much more realistic predictor of success.

Key point

At Welton, youth is seen as a precious resource, but only when it is threatened. When it is healthy and protected, youth is seen as an immature and unfocused stage in life, which must be pushed through in order to achieve manhood and success.

Q What different views of youth are shown in the film and with which do you agree?

Q How does the historical context of the film affect how Neil's death would have been viewed?

Q What role does class play in forming the way in which the various characters view youth?

Literature is alive

Key quotes

> No matter what anybody tells you, words and ideas can change the world. (s.3; Mr Keating to his class)
>
> Poetry can come from anything with the stuff of revelation in it. (s.3; Mr Keating to his class)

Perhaps the most important theme of the film is the debate about the role literature should play in the emotional life of its readers. This theme is reflected in the title of the film and is the genesis of the titular society whose revival drives the dramatic action. Mr Keating's main goal as a teacher is to bring literature, specifically poetry, to life for his students. He wants to show them how it can be relevant to their emotional lives, rather than simply an academic requirement. The other teachers show concern that the boys are not emotionally equipped to explore the adult and complex themes that arise in literature, and instead believe that boys of this age benefit from rote memorisation, e.g. Mr McAllister says to Mr Keating incredulously, 'Free thinkers at seventeen?' (s.3). It is notable that, before becoming headmaster, Mr Nolan taught the same subject as Mr Keating. When he reminisces about teaching (s.8), it is implied that he, too, feels strongly about the power and value of literature. It seems that everyone at Welton acknowledges the importance (and indeed, the possible danger) of literature; the disagreement is about the most suitable way to teach it.

Thematically, the ability to engage with and benefit from reading literature becomes symbolic of a true enjoyment of life and an emotional awakening. Mr Keating is keen to point out that it is important to go about the day-to-day business of life, but that literature is, as he puts it, 'what we stay alive for' (s.3). In this regard, Neil does not interpret Mr Keating's teachings entirely as intended. Neil's suicide implies that he feels that a life in which the arts and literature are not valued is no life at all, whereas Mr Keating is also careful to say, 'Medicine, law, business, engineering, these are noble pursuits' (s.3). His age allows him to take a more balanced and less extreme position on the value of literature.

Because literature is portrayed as vibrant and valuable in the film, the act of writing is seen, by extension, as an even further fulfilment of human potential. It is notable that both Knox and Todd write original pieces, while Neil – who is passionate about Mr Keating's ideas but, in the end, unable to follow through on them (unable to express his feelings to his father when invited to do so) – instead chooses an art form (acting) in which he speaks text written by someone else. The most basic and creative literary endeavour, writing, doesn't appeal to Neil in the way it does to the other boys. This implies that he may in fact be using the Dead Poets Society as a way to avoid confronting his feelings about his father and the life that has been chosen for him. Todd, on the other hand, is painfully honest and interior in his writing, preferring not to speak, write or read at all unless it is from his heart.

Key points

Literature represents emotional awareness, self-knowledge and the ability to fully experience life.

The fullest experience of literature is not only to read and absorb values, but also to attempt to add 'a verse' oneself and experience the value of creation.

Valuing literature does not mean devaluing other enterprises, but rather acknowledging the emotional and spiritual aspects of life in addition to the practical and rational.

Q What is the importance of the scene in which Mr Keating covers Todd's eyes and forces him to describe the madman?

Q In what sense does the Dead Poets Society help the boys 'seize the day' and make the most of their young lives? How does reading poetry give them an experience in their lives that they don't get from other activities?

DIFFERENT INTREPRETATIONS

Interpreting a text

Different interpretations arise from different responses to a text. Over time, a text will give rise to a wide range of responses from its readers, who may come from various social or cultural groups and live in very different places and historical periods. These responses can be published in newspapers, journals and books by critics and reviewers, or they can be expressed in discussions amongst readers in the media, classrooms, book groups and so on. While there is no single correct reading or interpretation of a text, it is important to understand that an interpretation is more than a personal opinion – it is the justification of a point of view on the text. To present an interpretation of the text based on your point of view you must use a logical argument and support it with relevant evidence from the text.

The critics' viewpoints

Dead Poets Society was well-received on its release. It was a commercial hit and received significant attention at the two main Hollywood awards ceremonies, the Golden Globe Awards and the Academy Awards.

Some negative reviews did criticise the script for having maudlin or emotionally manipulative aspects. However, Weir's direction and the performances of the young actors were both almost universally praised, with Rita Kempley of the *Washington Post* acknowledging the young cast as 'a dazzling ensemble of persuasive newcomers' (Kempley, 1989). Reviews of Robin Williams' performance as John Keating were polarised, with strong praise as well as disappointed criticism from those who felt Williams was unable to break out of his comedic styling. Noted critic Roger Ebert condemned the film for 'pandering to adolescent audiences' and putting forward 'pious platitudes masquerading as a courageous stand' (Ebert, 1989). Ebert's review was one of the most negative that the film received.

The most positive reviews praised Weir's style, with Richard Schickel noting that, 'director Weir, who is good at unspoken menace (*Picnic at Hanging Rock* and *The Last Wave*), has created a subtly dark and claustrophobic atmosphere' (Schickel, 1989). The *Washington Post* lauded Weir for his creation of Mr Keating, whom Kempley describes as 'More than a breath of fresh air' (Kempley, 1989). The same critic later refers to 'the joys of Keating's classroom'.

Schickel, in particular, praised the film overall, noting '[Robin Williams] and the movie deserve attention, respect and finally gratitude' (Schickel, 1989).

Two interpretations

Interpretation 1: *Dead Poets Society* asserts the value of independent thinking by young people

By focusing on the fate of the character Todd, Weir illustrates the transformative effect that modern teaching methods, including treating students as intellectual equals, can have on young people.

Early in the film, Todd is presented as painfully shy, unable to interact comfortably even with the boys who welcome him openly and with acceptance. Despite spending all night trying to write a poem, his crippling fear of being the centre of attention causes him to fail to complete the assignment (s.6). It is at this point, however, that Mr Keating chooses to push him beyond his comfort zone, having seen potential and intelligence in him, even when Todd gave little outward indication of these traits. Keating covers Todd's eyes in an attempt to allow him to express himself without having to face the class. This scene not only illustrates Todd's potential, but also Keating's keen understanding of his students. Weir highlights the impact attentive teachers can have when they believe in their students enough to challenge them to use their latent or untapped talents.

Additionally, many critics have noted that Neil's suicide as a reaction to the clash between ideals stirred up in him by Mr Keating and the pressures exerted on him by his father is 'somewhat implausible'

(Schickel, 1989). Given that Neil showed no signs of depression or self-harm prior to his suicide, it can be interpreted as more of a metaphorical touch by Weir than a literal death, an interpretation that all the more strongly supports the idea that Mr Keating's teachings (and the teachings of similarly inspiring educators) certainly offer far more benefit than harm. Todd's reaction to Keating's teachings seems to be a more literal and plausible representation of the effects of modern and interactive teaching philosophies. Also, Todd's storyline acknowledges the ability of students to deal with even those philosophies that are challenging to them. Their learning process is described as a kind of 'groping with energetic sobriety toward an idea' (Schickel, 1989), implying that the students, when prompted, are willing to put in effort and rise to the task of understanding unfamiliar concepts, when they are presented with passion and in a relevant manner (as is done by Mr Keating).

Todd is shown to be able to carry, albeit in small ways, the positive influence of Mr Keating's teachings into all realms of his life, while Neil is unable to do so, only succeeding in living up to his Romantic ideals while within the protected space of Welton Academy. Todd, on the other hand, is able to question Mr Nolan even when his parents are present, asking, 'What's gonna happen to Mr Keating?' (s.9). This small act of defiance, unthinkable from the Todd the viewer sees in the opening scenes, shows that he has truly changed. Similarly, he stands up to Cameron, not confrontationally as Charlie does, but morally, saying, 'That's not true, Cameron, you know that. [Mr Keating] didn't put us up to anything. Neil loved acting' (s.9). Todd at this point has made the transition from being meek and ineffectual to a true believer in justice and self-determinism. This also explains his extreme reaction to Neil's death – he is unwilling to believe Neil would devalue life by taking his own, as life was, according to Mr Keating's teachings, the most precious resource. It is at this point that Todd himself realises that he has more successfully internalised the philosophy of the Dead Poets Society and Mr Keating than Neil, and the viewer realises it along with him.

In particular, Weir demonstrates his intention to show Mr Keating's positive influence and highlight Todd's narrative, not only by ending the film with a Todd-centric scene but also making Todd's face the final shot, indicating that his emotional and intellectual journey is the most important aspect of the film.

Interpretation 2: *Dead Poets Society* concludes that adolescents are unequipped to handle the emotional burden of individualism and that treating students as the intellectual equals of their teachers can be naïve and unfair to minds that require guidance rather than free rein.

By focusing on the character of Neil, Weir issues a warning about the dangers of idealism when combined with a lack of emotional maturity, and reminds teachers and educators that treating students as intellectual equals may be more cruel than kind. A minor character, Mr McAllister, is included to serve as the voice of reason between the extremes of Mr Nolan and Mr Keating.

Rita Kempley writes in the *Washington Post,* 'Marching to one's own drummer proves near-impossible when the approval-givers have got the drumsticks' (Kempley, 1989). With this interpretation, Mr Keating is setting students like Neil up for conflict by encouraging them to follow their own desires, which will inevitably clash with those of their parents. Whether this conflict can be resolved positively is questionable. Neil's fate illustrates a worst-case scenario, in which the conflict becomes irresolvable for the young person and he is utterly unable to deal with the situation. Neil is encouraged to embrace idealistic philosophies by Mr Keating, but he doesn't have the emotional preparation to then engage in the resulting conflict, as is illustrated by his inability to answer his father when he is finally – albeit hostilely – invited to state what he wants (s.9).

Vincent Canby, writing in the *New York Times*, noted that Mr Keating's inability to predict the extremity of Neil's reaction makes Keating 'seem more of a dubious fool' (Canby, 1989). Canby concludes that, in the context of the film, it is inevitable that 'one of [Mr Keating's] students will take his teachings to some fatal length ... the Keating character is far more culpable than either he or the movie realises'. The culpability of Mr Keating is key to understanding Weir's intent and his interpretation of the screenplay. If Keating should have been able to observe and understand Neil with the same insight and accuracy with which he observed Todd, he is indeed partially responsible for Neil's death and the film is therefore a cautionary tale about exposing young people to philosophies for which they may not be emotionally prepared. Critic Desson Howe, also of the *Washington Post*, sums up this conflict, saying, 'most romantic flights of fancy inevitably crash-land' (Howe, 1989).

Mr McAllister is an important character, because without him the viewer would be forced to choose between the idealistic Mr Keating and the cynical Mr Nolan. Knowing that few others would agree with the harsh headmaster, Weir and Schulman included the character of Mr McAllister to showcase a possible middle ground that may be more beneficial to students. McAllister is able to absorb some of the more positive aspects of Keating's style (he is seen taking his students outside during lessons near the end of the film [s.9]). He views his students as capable but impressionable, in need of guidance and encouragement but ill-equipped to practice delayed gratification or long-term thinking. Weir chooses to highlight their differing philosophies in an explicit conversation, early in the film, in order to make it clear to viewers that there are other options than those Keating chooses. McAllister even explicitly states he is 'not a cynic' (s.3), showing that, although he is not entirely aligned with Keating's beliefs, he still cares deeply about the students in his classes.

Weir's focus on Neil is clear from the amount of screen time that the character receives, as well as the focus on Neil in the film's climax. The most emotionally charged scene is that of Neil's death, showing that the greatest impact and strongest influence of Mr Keating's teachings is played out in Neil's narrative.

QUESTIONS & ANSWERS

This section focuses on your own analytical writing on the text and gives you strategies for producing high-quality responses in your coursework and exam essays.

Essay writing – an overview

An essay is a formal and serious piece of writing that presents your point of view on the text, usually in response to a given essay topic. Your 'point of view' in an essay is your interpretation of the meaning of the text's language, structure, characters, situations and events, supported by detailed analysis of textual evidence.

Analyse – don't summarise

In your essays it is important to avoid simply summarising what happens in a text:

- A **summary** is a description or paraphrase (retelling in different words) of the characters and events. For example: 'Macbeth has a horrifying vision of a dagger dripping with blood before he goes to murder King Duncan'.
- An **analysis** is an explanation of the real meaning or significance that lies 'beneath' the text's words (or images in a film). For example: 'Macbeth's vision of a bloody dagger shows how deeply uneasy he is about the violent act he is contemplating – as well as his sense that supernatural forces are impelling him to act'.

A limited amount of summary is sometimes necessary to let your reader know which part of the text you wish to discuss. However, always keep this to a minimum and follow it immediately with your analysis (explanation) of what this part of the text is really telling us.

Plan your essay

Carefully plan your essay so that you have a clear idea of what you are going to say. A plan will ensure that your ideas flow logically, that your argument remains consistent and that you stay on the topic. An essay plan should be a list of **brief dot points** – no more than half a page. It includes:

- your central argument or main contention – a concise statement (usually in a single sentence) of your overall response to the topic. See 'Analysing a sample topic' for guidelines on how to formulate a main contention.
- three or four dot points for each paragraph indicating the main idea and evidence/examples from the text. Note that in your essay you will need to *expand* on these points and *analyse* the evidence.

Structure your essay

An essay is a complete, self-contained piece of writing. It has a clear beginning (the introduction), middle (several body paragraphs) and end (the last paragraph or conclusion). It should also have a central argument that runs throughout, linking each paragraph to form a coherent whole.

See examples of introductions and conclusions in the 'Analysing a sample topic' and 'Sample answer' sections.

The introduction establishes your overall response to the topic. It includes your main contention and outlines the main evidence you will refer to in the course of the essay. Write your introduction *after* you have done a plan and *before* you write the rest of the essay.

The body paragraphs argue your case – they present evidence from the text and explain how this evidence supports your argument. Each body paragraph needs:

- a strong **topic sentence** (usually the first sentence) that states the main point being made in the paragraph
- **evidence** from the text, including some brief quotations
- **analysis** of the textual evidence explaining its significance and **explanation** of how it supports your argument
- **links back to the topic** in one or more statements, usually towards the end of the paragraph.

Connect the body paragraphs so that your discussion flows smoothly. Use some linking words and phrases like 'similarly' and 'on the other hand', but don't start every paragraph like this. Another strategy is to use a significant word from the last sentence of one paragraph in the first sentence of the next.

Use key terms from the topic – or synonyms for them – throughout, so the relevance of your discussion to the topic is always clear.

The conclusion ties everything together and finishes the essay. It includes strong statements that emphasise your central argument and provide a clear response to the topic.

Avoid simply restating the points made earlier in the essay – this will end on a very flat note and imply that you have run out of ideas and vocabulary. The conclusion is meant to be a logical extension of what you have written, not just a repetition or summary of it. Writing an effective conclusion can be a challenge. Try using these tips:

- Start by linking back to the final sentence of the second-last paragraph – this helps your writing to 'flow', rather than just leaping back to your main contention straight away.
- Use synonyms and expressions with equivalent meanings to vary your vocabulary. This allows you to reinforce your line of argument without being repetitive.
- When planning your essay, think of one or two broad statements or observations about the text's wider meaning. These should be related to the topic and your overall argument. Keep them for the conclusion, since they will give you something 'new' to say but still follow logically from your discussion. The introduction will be focused on the topic, but the conclusion can present a wider view of the text.

Essay topics

1. Is Mr Keating's influence on the boys positive or negative? How do you justify your answer?
2. What is Todd's role in the film? Why is he an important character?
3. Neil's suicide comes as a surprise to the other characters. Discuss.
4. Why is so little known about Mr Keating's personal background? Why might the director have chosen to reveal little about the character as an individual?

5 Are the other boys (Charlie, Knox, Meeks, Cameron and Pitts) fully realised characters? What is their experience of Mr Keating as a teacher?
6 Is Mr Perry a manipulative man who needs to be in control or a father who wants the best for his son?
7 What is the role of poetry in *Dead Poets Society*? Why are the particular poems that are included chosen?
8 How does Neil's death affect Mr Keating?
9 Several of the characters embrace Mr Keating's *carpe diem* mantra, with a variety of consequences. Discuss.
10 What is the role of the natural world in *Dead Poets Society*?

Useful vocabulary for writing about *Dead Poets Society*

Cut: This is a basic film term that refers to the transition from scene to scene (when the location changes abruptly on screen). For instance, a scene in a restaurant may cut to a scene in a school, without expressly explaining how the characters moved from one place to another. Cuts are used for narrative economy. There are different kinds of cuts, including a 'jump cut' (which is jarring to the viewer and draws attention to the difference between two scenes), 'cross cut' (to show two different events that are occurring at the same time in different locations) and a 'match cut' (the opposite of a jump cut, it aims for seamless transition, not drawing attention to the change of scene).

Diegetic and non-diegetic sound: These are film terms referring to the two different kinds of sound and music that may appear in a movie. The source of diegetic sound is visible on the screen or is implied by the action of the film, such as characters' voices, sounds made by objects or actions in the film. Non-diegetic sound occurs as part of the aesthetic of the film: the characters would not be able to hear it – it is not actually part of the action of the film, but is only audible to the viewer (most songs and music fall into this second category, unless they are played as part of the action of the film).

Foreshadowing: Foreshadowing is a technique used by writers and directors to subtly inform the viewer or reader of an important event that will occur later in the plot. Foreshadowing can take many forms; it may be in words or images, and will often go unnoticed until after the narrative event it predicts has passed, e.g. childless characters might notice a pregnant woman on the street, foreshadowing their own upcoming, unexpected parenthood; or a character might pass a train station or airport, foreshadowing travel.

Romantic and Romanticism: In the literary sense, Romantic (with a capital R) does not refer to romantic love between two people, but rather to an emotional and individual approach to art and life. Romanticism emerged as a reaction to rationalism and the Enlightenment. Romanticism values individual experience and input and was popular from the mid-eighteenth century to the late-nineteenth century, with movements in literature, visual art and music. Some of the most famous artists of the Romantic Movement were: Keats, Byron, Shelley and Wordsworth (literature); Chopin, Liszt and Tchaikovsky (music); and Delacroix and Goya (visual art). Romanticism championed the subjective over the objective, and valued the individual over the collective. Romantic works also valued the natural world and its effect on the human spirit. The Romantic concern with a single character or viewpoint in a particular piece of literature remains common in contemporary writing.

Analysing a sample topic

What is Todd's role in the film? Why is he an important character?
This topic asks you to look at the character of Todd and the role his presence serves in the film, thematically and practically. Read the sample question carefully, and note that it has two parts: the first asks about Todd's role; the second asks why Todd is important, meaning his character has significant impact on either the other characters, the plot, the viewer, or all of the aforementioned.

Think about when and how Todd enters the narrative, how he is portrayed as a writer and poet himself and what lessons he learns during the course of the film.

Sample introduction

The character of Todd is important both as an observer of the action and a participant who is changed by the action. He serves to illustrate the transformative power of poetry and literature, and therefore communicates the film's central thesis.

Body paragraph 1

Todd is the first character among the boys to have a spoken line and to be shown alone, highlighting his importance and the importance of his journey and change.

- Mention that Todd's first line is 'Thank you' (s.1), communicating his nature as responsive and reactive rather than active at the beginning of the film.
- Note that Todd is shown alone in his room, unlike the other boys, giving him an interiority that is not shown in the others (s.2).
- Examine how Todd's parents behave towards him in the opening scene, in contrast to how Neil's father behaves, and how these different kinds of relationships could affect the two boys' emotional states.

Body paragraph 2

While all the boys embrace the Dead Poets Society, Todd alone becomes a creator and writes and reads his own work, showing that he benefits the most from the society and Mr Keating's teachings.

- Reference how seriously Todd takes the original composition assignment, in particular the scene in which he is shown to have stayed up all night (s.6).
- Examine Todd's spontaneous composition (the sweaty-toothed madman poem he creates in s.6) and what it communicates about him as a character.
- Discuss the significance of Todd writing 'Seize the day!' in his notebook (s.2).

Body paragraph 3

Todd is the first boy to stand on his own and defy Mr Nolan to honour Mr Keating in the final scene, showing that he is the character who has grown and changed most dramatically.

- Reference Todd's reluctance to sign the document implicating Mr Keating, as well as his accusation that Cameron knows Mr Keating is not responsible for Neil's death (s.9).
- Examine the shots of Todd's face early in the final scene, before he works up the courage to address Mr Nolan and prior to his standing on the desk (s.10) and what his expression says about his internal narrative.
- Discuss how Todd and Neil are different and how they are similar, and why they react differently to Mr Keating's teachings.

Sample conclusion

At the beginning of the film, Todd's role is mainly as an observer of the main action (particularly the conflict between Neil's desires and his family pressures). This role allows for commentary on the action, making Todd the voice of the film's themes and teachings. However, by the end of the film he moves from observer to participant, mirrored in his move from a reader to writer of poetry, thereby summarising and exemplifying all of Mr Keating's teachings.

SAMPLE ANSWER

What is the role of the natural world in *Dead Poets Society*?

The natural world in *Dead Poets Society* represents the freedom and self-awareness of individualism and Romantic ideals. It is an environment that encourages the natural and impulsive nature of childhood, while also encouraging the active self-determinism of adulthood. As a free space, it is also a space that may be dangerous, since the freedom to make one's own decisions opens up the possibility of danger, compared with the safety of a more structured world. The natural world is a space where the characters are most able to access their inner selves and get in touch with their desires, especially the desires that are discouraged in more structured settings. In this sense, in *Dead Poets Society* the outdoor world is representative of the true self, with all its inherent possibilities and dangers.

The natural world is of particular significance to the character of Neil, who is the first to suggest reconvening the Dead Poets Society. When Mr Keating mentions that the society used to meet, in his day, at 'the old Indian cave' (s.3), Neil is the only student who immediately knows the location to which he is referring, which implies Neil alone has explored the grounds around the school and has already sought comfort from the natural world before the film opens. As a contrast, Cameron says, 'I don't know, it's starting to sound dangerous' (s.3). His discomfort with the natural world is a reflection of his discomfort with any environment that lacks the order and structure of Welton and similar institutions.

When Neil makes the decision to end his life, he again turns to the natural world for one last genuine experience, opening the windows of his parents' house wide, allowing the cold winter air in. He also removes most of his clothing, so that his body is in a similarly natural state. He symbolically leaves the crown of branches on the windowsill (s.9), implying that it is a kind of death for him to be forced to part with the natural, impulsive, instinctive world (represented for Neil by acting), and a physical death must naturally follow. His view of the natural world is contrasted with Todd's. Todd also reaches out to nature in a time of crisis: when he receives news of Neil's death, he runs outside (s.9). However, Todd views the natural world as a refuge while for Neil it is a source of inspiration for his Romantic ideals. As the film progresses, Todd is seen outside more often, despite the dropping temperatures. This represents his growing ease with himself; if both Neil and Todd see their true selves in the outdoor world, then Todd sees a growing sense of self-worth and confidence, while Neil sees a growing sense of conflict and danger. It is his embracing of this danger, the end of this conflict, which is represented in his suicide.

The final and notable reference to the natural world in the film takes place after Neil's death. We see Mr Keating inside his room, separated from nature; his mourning process is the opposite of Todd's, who has only recently awoken to the benefits of the natural world. Mr Keating has become, probably temporarily, afraid of the natural world and what it represents: the unpredictable, the passionate and the impulsive – characteristics that were evident in Neil and contributed to his actions. Mr Keating is not only inside the school, but upstairs in his small, dark room. Mr McAllister, however, is shown outside in the snow with his students (s.9). He is the character who has managed to find a balance between the natural and civilised worlds, drawing inspiration from Mr Keating's methods (in taking his students outside and illustrating Latin vocabulary by pointing out things on campus) but remaining conservative in his attitudes – still teaching in a traditional lecture-based manner. In this sense, Weir communicates the message that no one can happily and peacefully live a life that is either entirely 'indoors' or entirely 'outdoors'. Like Mr McAllister, people must strive to find a balance.

By showing the natural world as a space that allows passionate and individualistic qualities to flourish, Weir presents the outdoors as a space where the characters are able to access their inner potential, whether the consequences be positive or negative. Weir contrasts the structured and civilised space of Welton Academy with frequent landscape and nature shots, including metaphorical shots of wild birds that represent the boys and their inner, wild potential.

REFERENCES & READING

Text

Weir, Peter, 1989. *Dead Poets Society*. Touchstone Pictures. Reissued 2006.

Script text

It is always useful to read the original script if it is available, as deviations from the script and other stylistic choices on the part of the director will be made obvious and of interest for thorough analysis. The DVD commentary with Weir, and other extra features on the DVD version of the film, can also be helpful resources in interpreting the film.

Schulman, Tom 2000, *Dead Poets Society: The Script Publishing Project*. Harvest Moon Publishing: Denver.

Further reading

While there is a wide range of personal interpretations available on the internet, there is not a significant body of professional critical work about *Dead Poets Society*. However, the film was widely reviewed by prominent critics; these professional reviews and their qualitative analysis of the film can be very helpful for academic analysis. It is useful to examine both positive and negative reviews of a film in order to understand varying interpretations. There are also several guides available for interpreting films generally that can be very useful, as well as some texts specifically examining Weir and his work as a whole.

Below are some texts about the film that may be helpful in analysing *Dead Poets Society*, as well as reviews of the film and texts about Weir's work.

Canby, Vincent 1989, 'Shaking Up a Boys' School With Poetry', *New York Times*, 2 June, http://movies.nytimes.com/movie/review?res=950DE0DE1F31F931A35755C0A96F948260&partner=Rotten%20Tomatoes/

Ebert, Roger 1989, 'Dead Poets Society', *Chicago Sun-Times,* 9 June, http://rogerebert.suntimes.com/apps/pbcs.dll/article?AID=/19890609/REVIEWS/906090301/1023/

Griffin, Nancy 1989, 'Poetry Man', *Premiere Magazine,* July, http://www.peterweircave.com/articles/articlec.html

Howe, Desson 1989, 'Dead Poets Society', *Washington Post,* 9 June, http://www.washingtonpost.com/wp-srv/style/longterm/movies/videos/deadpoetssocietypghowe_a0b21e.htm/

Kempley, Rita 1989, 'Dead Poets Society', *Washington Post,* 9 June, http://www.washingtonpost.com/wp-srv/style/longterm/movies/videos/deadpoetssocietypgkempley_a09fc4.htm/

Kleinbaum, Nancy H 1997, *Dead Poets Society: Additional Texts for Study at School,* Aschendorff, *Münster.*

LLC Books 2010, *Films Directed by Peter Weir (Study Guide): Green Card, Witness, Dead Poets Society, the Year of Living Dangerously, Fearless, the Truman Show,* LLC Books, Memphis.

Schickel, Richard 1989, 'Cinema: A Bothered School Spirit', *TIME Magazine,* 5 June, http://www.time.com/time/magazine/article/0,9171,957853,00.html/

Thomson, David 2010, *The New Biographical Dictionary of Film,* 5th edn, Knopf, New York.